# Stage by Stage

# Stage by Stage

## A Handbook for Using Drama in the Second Language Classroom

Ann F. Burke and Julie O'Sullivan

HEINEMANN
Portsmouth, NH

**Heinemann**
A division of Reed Elsevier Inc.
361 Hanover Street
Portsmouth, NH 03801–3912
www.heinemanndrama.com

*Offices and agents throughout the world*

**Library of Congress Cataloging-in-Publication Data**
Burke, Ann F.
    Stage by stage : a handbook for using drama in the second language classroom / Ann F. Burke and Julie O'Sullivan.
        p.   cm.
    Includes bibliographical references.
    ISBN 0-325-00380-7
    1. English language—Study and teaching—Handbooks, manuals, etc.   2. Drama in education—Handbooks, manuals, etc.
    I. O'Sullivan, Julie.   II. Title.
    PE1128.A2 B856 2002
    428′.0071—dc21                                                2002005080

*Editor: Lisa A. Barnett*
*Production service: Lisa Garboski, bookworks*
*Production coordinator: Elizabeth Valway*
*Cover design: Jenny Jensen Greenleaf*
*Typesetter: House of Equations, Inc.*
*Manufacturing: Steve Bernier*

Printed in the United States of America on acid-free paper
06 05 04 03 02 DA 1 2 3 4 5

From Ann F. Burke:
To a favorite teacher: Donald C. Eyssen

From Julie O'Sullivan:
To Mum and Dad

# Contents

# Foreword

To open this book is to open an invitation to stir the imagination. Ann Burke and Julie O'Sullivan have brought their love of teaching, drama, and fun together in a book that brings drama to the English as a Second Language (ESL) classroom, making it accessible to both students and teachers. Drama offers language learners the opportunity to use their imaginations while learning. The use of improvisation, role-plays, and scripted texts provides a setting in which learners take on roles outside themselves allowing them to experiment unselfconsciously with language and vocabulary, pronunciation, intonation and voice, gestures, and body movement in ways that they have not experienced before—especially not in a language classroom!

*Drama* may seem like a weighty and serious word. To think of it as beyond reach would be to miss the fun. The use of drama is a way to encourage language learning through combining dialogue and action, and it is approached gradually in this book through role-play, small skits, and scripts. The authors' experiences in acting, directing, and ESL teaching combine to make this book a useful tool for teachers with no acting or drama experience as well as for more experienced teachers.

This book can be used in multiple ways. Burke and O'Sullivan encourage teachers to "dip in" to the book to use individual activities. The drama activities, with their range of emphasis and their integration of skills, can be used to supplement many different ESL classes. Pronunciation or listening-speaking classes benefit from the contextualized focus on pronunciation, use of voice, and intonation inherent in performing. Even beginning-level learners can get in on the learning fun. An ingenious set of role-plays asks learners to convey emotion and meaning by adding intonation to a single word, something within the reach of all learners. The activities in the book can also be used in a reading course by bringing texts to life. Going beyond the more familiar practice of discussing the meaning of a text, learners use the activities in this book to interpret a text not only with their developing reading skills, but also with their voices, their bodies, and their actions. In some activities the learners follow improvised role-plays with scripting their own dialogues, excellent for an emphasis on oral and written language production as well as interpretation. In addition, the negotiation of meaning that accompanies pair and group work with the drama activities results in tangible outcomes such as the production of a skit or the writing of a script that make the activities appropriate to any language class.

Once teachers and students experience the fun of dipping into Burke and O'Sullivan's exercises, they are very likely to want to do more, and the authors provide that, too. This book also serves as the primary text for an ESL drama class, moving from drama exercises, to role-plays, to the selection of appropriate scripts for learners, and for the most ambitious students and teachers, the production of a play.

Fun is serious business with Burke and O'Sullivan as they lead the way to greater language learning opportunities through drama. So, roll up your sleeves, and get ready to enjoy the teaching and learning process as you and your students experience the advantages of working with drama in the ESL classroom.

*Kathleen Bardovi-Harlig*
*Indiana University,*
*Bloomington, Indiana*

# Acknowledgments

We wish to thank the following people for believing in this book: Our students over the years who participated in our drama classes and with their enthusiasm joined in the creative and linguistic endeavor. All our friends and colleagues at the Center for English Language Training at Indiana University for their interest and encouragement. Kathleen Bardovi-Harlig for her good advice. Cindy Trisler for reading an early draft. Bill Johnston for reading the whole manuscript. Lisa Barnett, our editor, for allowing us to write the book we wanted. Our family and friends for their patience. Last but not ever least, Richard and Elliott for their starring roles!

# Introduction

## Why Have We Written This Book?

We want to encourage teachers to use drama and role-play in the classroom. We also want to assure teachers that they do not have to be trained as actors or have any prior experience in the theater. Drama is simply a good way to get students' whole selves involved with language and it is fun. Some administrators fear that anything outside the set curriculum is frivolous, but we wish to assure anyone who picks up this book and tries these activities that they are anything but frivolous. In drama and role-play exercises teachers can work on elements (such as pronunciation, cultural pragmatics, or nonverbal communication) that often they have little time for in class and the students discover that they are having fun while learning.

We have looked around for a book that would introduce drama in a teacher-friendly way. We want a book small enough to carry around without breaking the teacher's back and one that the teacher can use easily. We want a book that has many activities for multiple levels, but also one that has small skits in it and that would help the neophyte teacher to tackle a staged production of a play. Since we haven't found such a book still in print that does all these things, we decided to write one.

## What Is Drama and Role-play?

First, we feel that we should make clear what we mean by drama and role-play.

## *Drama*

For the purposes of this book, drama is a way of infusing excitement into classroom exercises by combining dialogue and action. Dialogue can be both invented language (improvising from students' active language) and interpreted language (acting a part in a play). And action is just that: putting whatever dialogue the students invent, write, or choose into motion. Drama includes acting exercises as well as performance preparation. In acting exercises, students experiment with how extralinguistic elements affect meaning: such things as how gestures "speak" or how pitch, speed, volume or pauses color the words. When working with scripts (from movies, television and stage), we use text analysis, rehearsals and performance to help the students interpret the language of a play. Text analysis gives students good reasons for reading in depth and rehearsals give students practice in speaking and listening and using their bodies to add to the interpretation. In rehearsals the students can also fine-tune pronunciation—something that other classes may ignore because of time constraints and the need to get at meaning—as a true communication goal. The reward of a good performance is that it is understood.

Acting out a play during a single class or in a series of classes can be done either for instructional purposes or for the enjoyment of the participants. The goal of working on a play does not necessarily have to be public performance: it can be a performance of one group within the class for all other classmates. Each teacher may decide that a goal is to acquaint students with literature or to illustrate a theme a class has been investigating or to give students practice in speaking and listening. However, if the students begin to show a desire to perform for an audience, we feel the teacher should be prepared to see the students through, keeping in mind that the process is what matters.

## *Role-play*

We use drama techniques such as role-play and improvisation to stimulate student-invented language. In role-play and improvisation, students create their own dialogues, using their active language and hopefully incorporating newly learned vocabulary and structures. Role-play is generally used to simulate the feel of a real-life situation in a classroom. Typically, in role-play, students are given a purpose, a situation, a setting, a goal (or goals), and a few directions. For instance, the purpose may be to practice inviting and responding to invitations; the situation may be that person A is alone and wants to go somewhere with someone; the setting may be A's dormitory, and one goal may be for A to get person B to say yes to a movie invitation; another goal may be for person B to politely say no. Typically, the instructor can give directions either vocally or on cards. The instructions are sometimes in the form of a command, for instance: "Ask student B . . ." that the students must change to "Would you like to . . . ?" or are sometimes a description of the situation, such as "You are a student. You want to . . ." and the students must invent what they would say in that situation.

Sample Role-Play Card: Following are two role-play cards. Student A does not know what is on student B's card.

A: You are a new student. You are lonely and would like to invite a classmate to go with you to the movies. Look at the newspaper ads to see what movies are playing and call B on the phone to see if B could go with you either on Thursday or Friday.

B: You are a student who is very busy. You play in the university orchestra and you have rehearsals on Wednesdays and Thursdays. You have a paper that is due on Monday and you have to go to the library to get more material, plus you have to allow time to finish writing the paper. Be polite, but firm in refusing A's invitation.

The role-play dialogue created by the students may be improvised for the moment (not written down) or written in script form to be used later for performance purposes. Mime (learning to use the body to express unspoken thoughts) is another form of role-play. This action without words does have a place in a language classroom because it shows students that movement carries subtle meanings and that sometimes body language can be in opposition to the words of the speaker (a friend asks the parent of a teenage driver, "Does your son have his driver's license yet?" The parent answers, "Yes," but scowls).

XV

# Should a Language Class Perform a Play?

## *Benefits to Students of a Theatrical Performance*

When we ask students to learn a part, we are asking them to do more than just memorize a lot of words. With the authentic speech models of characters in a good play, students are exposed to language that is more complex than what exists in their own "active language." They must first understand and then interpret—put sounds and gestures together to express what a playwright has written. And when students memorize, rehearse, and perform a playwright's work, they *internalize* good models of the language they wish to learn. Internalizing grammatical forms, phrases, vocabulary, and language rhythms is not very likely when students work with minimal pairs or single sentences isolated in pronunciation exercises, but is possible when they memorize a stream of language in a play dialogue and rehearse it a number of times.

## The role of memorization in drama

In preparing to perform a play, actors have to memorize the words in a dramatic text. However, they do not try to remember simply the words; they need to understand the context as well. Second language learners memorize lines in the same manner as professional actors and have the added benefit of internalizing the new forms of the second language in the process.

- Before memorizing lines, students read the text very carefully and interpret the meaning. Once students feel they understand what is happening on the surface (the words that are spoken) and underneath (what is not said), they can begin to work on conveying meaning verbally through pronunciation, stress, and intonation, and nonverbally through gestures, facial expressions, and body posture. It is only after students know the text very well that they are ready to memorize their lines.
- After students have memorized the words of a play, they grasp a deeper meaning behind the words because they have "lived" the context. Perhaps this can best be illustrated through

describing one student's epiphany. Raul had a small part in *Twelve Angry Jurors*. The students had been rehearsing and had been off-book (working without the text in front of them) for a couple weeks. One day, after Raul had said one of his lines, he suddenly shouted, "I have the most important line in the play!" We asked him what he meant and he said excitedly that he had just realized that the remainder of the play turned on those few words. He had been saying those lines for several weeks, but when the words were truly his through memorization and he was attempting to breathe life into them, the meaning finally became clear to him.

- From a practical point of view, once students have memorized their lines and no longer need to hold the text in their hands for security, they are free to work with the language at a deeper level. They can concentrate on bringing out subtle meanings and nuances in the words themselves. In addition, students can more easily portray their character by experimenting with facial expressions, gestures, posture, and movement because the lines are in their heads and no longer just in the book they are holding. In regular language classes, there is very little time to work on verbal and nonverbal communication in such depth.

## Pronunciation

Plays are written as spoken language and not language to be read silently. Therefore, actors have to work intensively on the sound of the words: pronunciation and prosody.

- Using drama in the second language classroom creates a real need for students to experiment with how to pronounce words in context. Students are working with large sections of text in a specific context and not words and sounds in isolation.
- Students are very motivated to say their lines correctly in order to be understood by an audience and to avoid looking foolish in public by mispronouncing their lines. For this reason, students are content when the teacher corrects their pronunciation during the rehearsal process.

* The ultimate goal of pronunciation practice in rehearsal is to work on the most problematic sounds of the various actors so that the audience can understand the play. Therefore, students should work with chunks of the text and concentrate on intonation and stress. If the teacher notices that a student has a problem that severely interferes with comprehension of the text, the teacher can assign that student minimal pair exercises (see Pronunciation Exercises, Chapter 2).

## Benefits to Students in Generating Their Own Scripts

In addition to benefiting from a theatrical performance, students also gain from writing their own scripts. We sometimes ask our students to write a script when we cannot find a play that fits our class' needs. In asking our students to write a play, we demand that students search and expand their abilities to express themselves. Students are often frustrated at their inability to say precisely what they want, and writing their own material helps them take some control over the situation. Whenever students write their own material, they have, it seems, zillions of questions about specific vocabulary items or phrasing, as in: "How do you say _____?" We once had a student who wanted her group to dramatize the signing of a wedding contract in her own country and she had very good reasons for arguing with the teacher when the word or words offered did not match the pictures she had in mind. Because she wanted to express an exact scene, she did not give up until she had found the words that helped her describe each facet of the occasion. She wanted the performers who were not from her own culture to be absolutely clear about what they were to say and act out for the other members of the class.

## Why Drama in the Classroom?

We believe that drama can be a very powerful tool in getting students to use the language. We are English as a Second Language professionals who have taught mostly at the university level. We have taught students from many different cultures and at many different language-learning levels. Over the years, we have used a variety of approaches. We have observed that it is in classes that use drama and role-play where a greater number of students become more confident and fluent.

## Drama Is One Key to Unlock Student Use of Language

We teachers don't always know what motivates particular students or what holds back their progress, but we should have on our key ring, keys to fit many locks. At one time in our program, we were using a series that integrated the major skills in a tightly controlled and coordinated approach. It was a generally successful series, but it did not allow time to incorporate a play performance into the curriculum, especially in the beginning levels. One year, we had one student whose lack of progress puzzled many of us. We shall call him Mohammed. Mohammed was a cheerful young man, but he was silent. He had transferred into our Intensive English Program from another school in the United States and had been placed in the beginning level (level 1). After fourteen weeks he hadn't said anything more than his name. He just sat and smiled. Some of us worried that he might have a hearing problem or that he might have suffered a trauma that silenced him, but in observing him outside of class, we could see that he talked to others in his native tongue.

In the middle of Mohammed's third time through level 1, the speaking skills teacher decided to insert a play into her work with the students. She gave Mohammed a part in it. To everyone's amazement, when the class in chorus began to repeat the lines, his voice was heard. He repeated the lines over and over, attempting to match the pitch, the speed and the emotion of the teacher's interpretation. He returned day after day with more lines memorized and after two weeks was able to give a spirited performance. We later discovered that he had a powerful motivation to begin to speak English. He was in love with a girl who was from a different culture (she was Japanese) who did not speak his language—English was the only way they could communicate. The classroom language had not inspired him to learn, but the language of the play had given him phrases that he could use in interpersonal exchanges.

## *Reasons to Try Drama and Role-play in the Language Class*

Aside from the pleasure such accomplishments give to us and to our students, there are sound reasons for using actors' methods in language classes.

1. Teachers and students can concentrate on pronunciation.
   Realizing that they must be understood, students feel less personally threatened when a teacher asks them to change or refine the way they pronounce certain sounds.

2. Students are motivated.
   One of the biggest reasons for including drama and role-play in our classrooms is student motivation. The teachers who have tried it have discovered that students forget that they should be learning and then do just that: learn by doing something they enjoy. And when students are having fun, they are open to acquiring skills and they feel comfortable experimenting with the new language. In turn, as they acquire skills they are more willing to continue learning.

3. Students are relaxed.
   Because the class seems less formal, the students relax. They are not restricted to their desks and are free to move around the class. Students are constantly interacting with each other, so they get to know one another well. They trust that others in the class will not ridicule them if they make a mistake. They also see that the teachers join in and may laugh at themselves when something goes funny. As a result, students gain confidence. They are more willing to take a risk with language out in the "real world" because they have been taking risks in the classroom and have been understood.

4. Students use language for real purposes.
   During the rehearsal process, we give many suggestions and directions. Students have to ask questions to make sure they understand the suggestions and to clarify directions. They need to negotiate with the director how to depict certain emotions, to consult with fellow actors on how and why the

plot develops as it does, and to discuss, with both director and actors, all sorts of stage business, such as where to stand and when to move.

5. Risk-taking equals heightened language retention.
   Students are taking a risk when they perform before their peers and will work hard because they do not want to make fools of themselves. There can be unpredictable moments in the performances of plays—an unexpected audience laugh or a forgotten line. These moments cause a tremendous rush of adrenaline—everyone on stage feels responsible for thinking or saying something that will carry the play forward. Anyone who has ever been in that situation knows that no one on stage at that moment is passive: every mind is engaged in trying to come up with the right set of words. This experience makes an indelible impression: they will never forget the connection between meaning and words of that particular situation. Ordinary classroom exchanges just do not have that kind of retention power. We also find that thinking quickly on one's feet transfers to real life interactions with native speakers.

6. Community is created.
   One of the most obvious benefits of a drama/role-play class is that students get to know each other better and even get to know their teacher better. Those teachers who direct their students in a play find out that they and the class interact more freely and, in turn, forge closer friendships than they would in most traditional classrooms.

7. Students and teachers can approach sensitive topics.
   There are some topics that students do not enter into easily. Plays about these topics can sometimes be a catalyst to an open and honest discussion that otherwise would stay locked within the students. Subjects such as death or suicide, betrayal of a confidence, or jealousy are painful, but if they can be discussed in relation to a character's reactions, they can help students examine them on an objective level.

## *Reasons That Teachers Do Not Try This Type of Class*

Unfortunately, many teachers fear and therefore avoid this type of class.

1. Teachers fear that they lack training in drama/role-play.
   Many of our colleagues have not had training in the theater and are not sure what to do or where to start. They have seen plays with complicated sets, costumes, lighting, and makeup. They feel inadequate to deal with those various technical aspects of theatrical presentation. We recommend they do the simplest kind of production: set the scene with words (narration). New teachers to drama are unsure of how to get the actors to move on stage. Once a colleague sat in with us as we started a rehearsal and was amazed how logically the movements grew out of the dialogue. "Oh, that's how it's done," she said. "It's easy. I had no idea." We hope to reassure you of that very fact.

2. Teachers fear that they cannot find teacher-friendly material.
   Teachers don't usually have a lot of time to hunt for plays that match their classes. They may have discovered some activities books or "how to put on a play" books or may have picked up a famous play, but none of these support the teacher throughout the whole process. We give you all that we feel a teacher needs: exercises and activities, a step-by-step process that includes text analysis (or a class-produced text), casting and rehearsal preparations through to a finished production plus a few scripts by the authors and a bibliography that will give you additional information on any one of these areas.

3. Teachers fear that the class will "get out of hand."
   In a role-play/drama class some of the teacher's authority is handed over to the students who then take responsibility for their own learning. We may all agree that this is a good thing to do, but when faced with a noisy group of students (who are practicing enthusiastically) we experience moments of uncertainty. For instance, during rehearsals leading up to a performance of scenes parodying the movie *Titanic,* our stu-

dents became very involved in their work. At one point, the teacher stopped interacting with the various groups rehearsing and just observed what was going on in the classroom. One student was practicing falling off a chair backwards into the arms of a colleague while a small group of classmates was directing both of the actors on the technicalities of how to safely do this and, at the same time, advising them about which version looked best. In another corner of the room, a female student was draped seductively across a table while her fellow actor moved around the table with an invisible paintbrush and pad of paper, pretending to paint an image of her; near them, a few classmates were making suggestions to the model about the best pose and to the painter on how to mime the strokes of the brush. Yet in another group one student was practicing swinging a paper axe attached to a wooden stick ninja-fashion; he was followed by each of the others in that group giving the axe a swing. The group was discussing one method and defending it over the others. To outsiders, the scene might have appeared to have no structure and they might have asked, "Are those students really learning?" If the observers would watch longer, it would become obvious that the teacher keeps control through moving from group to group and interacting with the students, thus keeping the students focused. We also encourage a teacher of this kind of class to establish (on the first or second day) ground rules that the whole group agrees to uphold: for example, respectful ways to disagree. The teacher could even type up the rules and procedures, so that if something goes wrong, everyone knows what to do. In such a class, many more of the students are speaking and listening than would be actively using the language in most traditional classrooms.

## How This Book Is Organized

This is a resource book. In Chapter 1 we describe a drama class, as opposed to more traditional language classes (reading literature, writing, speaking, and listening). In this chapter we talk about setting the atmosphere of the class, and include many exercises that help the students get acquainted and that create a relaxed environment. We give you a list of stage terms that your class should know before they even look at a script. We suggest how to organize such a class.

In the second chapter, we focus on the type of exercises that acting classes use to improve voice qualities, to examine what is most expressive in gesture and body language.

In Chapter 3, we list considerations that should be taken into account when choosing a play for your class. We also list sources for finding plays. And we guide you through developing your own text for performance.

In Chapter 4, after you have chosen a text to work with, we take you step by step through text analysis, casting and rehearsals, and the practical aspects of performing a play.

In each chapter, we mention how drama and role-play can be used in skills (writing, reading, and speaking) classes. Some of you will not have the opportunity to do a complete class on drama and role-play; however, we wish to encourage you to incorporate these methods into your regular classes.

In Appendix 2, we even provide you with several Burke/O'Sullivan miniskits. In the bibliography, we have listed actors' scene books that have short scenes from full-length plays that can be used with learners of a second language. Also in the bibliography we have annotated books that relate to various areas we cover in this book. Some of these are out of print, but may be found in your local library; some of them you should have in your personal library, and others should be included in a departmental library for general use of your faculty.

## For Whom Is This Book Written?

We have written this book for the many teachers who would like to use drama in their classes, but either for lack of training or frustration in finding material, have stayed away from it. Because of our background in English as a Second Language, we have tried drama at all levels, even very beginning classes, of ESL in a university setting; however, we believe that teachers of any language, whether in secondary schools or colleges, can adapt the exercises and methods for their own classes. And no theatrical training is necessary, just a willingness to be flexible.

## How Can This Book Be Used?

This is a dip-into–type book. We know that some teachers will want a few dialogues that they can work with in class. Some will use the activities/exercises. Others may need the guidance of how to put on a play. Still others will want the bibliography to find more recommended material. (We note in the bibliography whether a book is for children or adults, and we note if there are scripts included.)

### *How to Use the Book with Different Levels*

Our drama experience has mainly been with teenage or adult learners at the intermediate or advanced level. The book can be used with lower levels as we outline below. Chapters 2 and 3 can be adapted for use with any level.

### Elementary level

**Type of text:** Short text or an extract from a longer text.
**Language work:** Work with surface level meaning and basic pronunciation to help with comprehension of the text.
**Nonverbal communication:** Either do not work on this or do some very basic work with gestures.
**Characterization:** Students can work with simple voices to portray a character—for example, a deep booming voice for an authority figure or a quiet voice for a subservient figure.
**Performance:** Students perform for each other and do not invite an outside audience to their performance.

### Intermediate level

**Type of text:** Work with skits or a one-act play.
**Language work:** Students try to understand the surface meaning and some of the underlying meaning of the text. Students work on intonation and stress when saying their lines and minimal pair work if necessary.

**Nonverbal communication:** Students work with gestures, facial expressions, posture and some movement.

**Characterization:** Students experiment with different voices and see how the character changes depending on the voice. In addition, they can work with the character's facial expressions and posture.

**Performance:** Students perform for one or two classes in the language program.

## Advanced level

**Type of text:** Skits, one-, two-, or three-act play.

**Language work:** Students conduct an in-depth reading of the text, looking at underlying meaning and nuances. Students experiment with intonation and stress to see how meaning is changed when using different patterns of prosody.

**Nonverbal communication:** Students try to bring out subtle nuances of meaning and characterization through facial expression, gestures, posture, mime, and movement.

**Characterization:** Students explore characters' emotions and how to portray relationships between the characters.

**Performance:** Students perform in front of a number of classes in the language program. We hope that teachers will acquaint themselves with the available material from the several disciplines we have used: language activities books, acting class texts, audition books, playwriting books, and play production texts. They can search their libraries for indexes and catalogues of published plays by professional playwrights, but they also should know that there are auditions books filled with short scenes that would be good for language practice. We hope that all teachers will make use of the parts of this book that address their particular needs.

# Chapter One

## Fluency and the Role of Drama in Language Classes

All teachers of a second language want their students to be fluent, but true fluency in language production doesn't happen all at once. For almost everyone, it takes a long time and much practice. In most language classes—even very small ones—teachers can rarely give each student the time to speak aloud more than a few sentences (and those sentences may or may not be part of a connected stream of thought). How then, do we as teachers encourage students to develop an easy flow of language? A teacher can affect students' progress to fluency by: 1. being enthusiastic, 2. being flexible, 3. making sure that students speak as much as the teacher does, 4. creating an atmosphere where students are not afraid of making mistakes, and 5. setting up a goal for the group.

### Teacher Enthusiasm

Enthusiasm is catching. Some exercises may suit your personality and others may not, but the students should never be able to detect the difference. Sometimes the way we present an exercise tells the students that we don't really think it will work. Never, never be tentative! Believe in yourself and what you are asking the students to do.

### Teacher Flexibility

In one class at any level, one approach may work fine; at the same level with another class, that approach may not. Basically, we suggest that you remain flexible and that you do not become discouraged when an exercise that you had liked on paper was not a roaring success. The next time you try it, it probably will be.

## Teacherspeak Versus Studentspeak

To become fluent, students must have a lot of speaking time. Fluency has to do with confidence in speaking, so you must let them speak. Like the old joke about how musicians can get to Carnegie Hall (they must practice), your students can't practice if you are speaking. Either you must get them to speak along with you (in chorus) or you must cut down on the minutes of time that you are speaking. Concentrated use of pronunciation exercises, choral repetitions, small group student interactions, pair work, as well as memorization of dialogues are essential elements in a drama class. Even students who can only produce very simple sentences can gain fluency (at that very simple level) if they practice those sentences enough.

## Relaxed Classroom Atmosphere

The teacher can help to create a relaxed atmosphere for everyone in the class. Students who fear making mistakes and feeling foolish in front of friends create a huge barrier to their own progress in second language learning. We have found that if the teachers join in the exercises, are not afraid to look silly while demonstrating, but are earnestly expecting the students to shed their inhibitions and imitate what the teacher is doing, most students will join in. We teachers can laugh at ourselves (Look what I'm willing to do in this class!) and explain that we are doing these things (maybe exaggeratedly) for instructional purposes.

## Performance: The Role of a Goal

Giving the students a goal of a performance of some sort is another important ingredient. Even at very beginning levels, the goal can be student memorization and performance for the teacher of practical phrases and sentences, such as where the student lives and what the student's telephone number is. Performing on a weekly basis helps the students feel that they have mastered some small aspects of the language; in turn, students retain sound flow and syntax in their mind's ear. In intermediate classes, groups can perform short skits for their classmates and at more advanced levels, students can carry off a full production for an invited audience. To illustrate the importance of such a goal, whenever we have staged a play or recorded radio plays, we have noticed that the students knew that they had to pay more attention than usual to pronunciation. They knew that they had to change faulty vowel or consonant sounds in order to be understood by an audience of their peers. The goal of being understood was always in the back of their minds and as a result, they were willing to work much harder than if they had had no such goal.

Here is another illustration of the importance of a goal. An actor from Eastern Europe married a local woman and came to this country before he learned English. Since his profession was acting, he longed to be active in theater again. He undertook a principal part in a local theatrical production within the first few weeks of arriving in our community. Coached by his wife, he memorized an enormous stream of English. He learned the structure of English grammar by countless repetitions of grammatically complex sentences. His wife assured him that he was communicating at the highest level, even though he did not thoroughly understand every phrase that he had memorized. His performance was exciting. The audience was aware that he spoke with an accent, but most people were totally unaware of his linguistic difficulties. He did not start at an easy level and build on it; he started by jumping into complicated structures and forcing them to come out of his mouth, much like opera singers learn an opera in the original language. Although he may have been uniquely motivated and gifted, we feel there is something to be learned from observing this actor's experience.

We learned that students can memorize structures they don't yet understand; they can recognize the situation that calls for that structure and they can connect the structure with the underlying meaning because the drama in which they encountered the structure has supplied them with that context.

In second language classes, we rarely ask students to memorize, even though many of our students come from cultures that

3

have demanded memorization throughout their school careers. In the past decade or so, memorization has actually been discouraged. The process of memorizing a part in a play for performance is different from rote memorizing for language classes. A theatrical rehearsal process requires students to use both their minds and bodies in a holistic way to convey the meaning of the words that they speak. They feel that they have experienced the words. Dramatic memorization can assist acquisition of complicated language structure and the "music" of a language (see Introduction for more details about memorization).

## Developing Fluency at Differing Levels

### Beginning Levels

In classrooms, learners of a second language usually begin by hearing and mimicking the sounds of that language while they make new connections between sound and meaning. Drama techniques such as choral repetitions or jazz chants are particularly good because everyone is speaking and no one is embarrassed in front of the class for not sounding good. Even though it is natural for teachers to worry that they may not be able to judge how each individual student is progressing, or that some students may not always be participating, our experience has been that students eagerly take part in choral work and that everybody gets lots of practice. Repetitions and memorization of material at this level are good ways to familiarize students with sound combinations of the new language. It gives the students a chance to work their tongues and lips around new combinations. It also helps internalize new grammar structures. For example, in English, adjectives come before nouns. Having students memorize sentences with many adjectives in front of nouns will help them internalize this structure. Putting these sentences into a dialogue will add context and something interesting for the students to hold onto.

Students need incentive to practice speaking when they are not in class. To encourage beginning-level students (who cannot sustain a conversation easily) to practice speaking outside of class hours, we have asked our students to memorize phrases, sentences, or dialogues that they have been saying in class. We set aside a time in class each week to hear the students orally "perform" memorized structures.

For practice, we ask them to say the sentences they wish to memorize before a mirror. They can watch how their lips, teeth, and tongue behave when they speak their "lines." We instruct them to try one of several methods that actors use to help themselves memorize

1. Recording cues on a tape recorder with blank spaces for responses, playing the cues over and over until they can supply the correct responses easily.

2. Writing the first letter of each word of the "line" that they want to remember—L b i f d = London Bridge is falling down.

3. Writing the first word and a series of dashes for the number of words that follow—London B___ i__ f___ d___.

As long as you do not ask them to memorize too much for any one homework assignment, this does not demand a lot of time and gives them a reason to review the work of the day (the grammar as well as the sound combinations they have encountered during classroom hours). In addition to familiarizing students with sound combinations, memorization helps students retain simple syntax. Consequently, students are less confused when a new phrase is introduced because they have an earlier one under control.

## Intermediate Levels

At the middle levels the students begin to shift from simple mimicry and classroom exercises to attempting to express ideas of their own. Because we teachers wish to encourage students to talk and to interact with other students, we do not always call attention to hesitations or to pronunciation faults in these attempts to express themselves so long as everyone in the class can unscramble meaning. We are very aware that the time to spend on each new phrase or sentence is limited. How do we give our students the necessary practice time to become familiar with new structures? Drama exercises can be a big help here. Students can use old structures and try out new ones in role-play. For example: teaching the present perfect and how it differs from the simple past can sometimes be a challenge. Let us assume that students have worked with the simple past and they are comfortably using it. We tell students that we use the present perfect in questions when the questioner is uncertain of the answer he will get. For example, if the questioner knows that his partner did something last night (saw a movie), he uses the simple past ("What movie did you see last night?"). However, if the questioner doesn't know if his partner saw a movie or when, he is more likely to use the present perfect ("Have you seen a movie lately?").

You could have students make up a small play working with the starting instructions:

*Student 1:* Ask Student 2 if he or she has been to New York. (*You don't know.*)

*Student 2:* Answer negatively and ask Student 1 if he or she has been to New York. (*You don't know the answer.*)

If Student 1 answers "No," then the questioners must continue asking about different cities until one of the students gets an affirmative answer.

**Scenario***: Students form questions based on the instructions given them.*

*Student 1:* "Have you been to New York?" (*Questioner is uncertain of the answer.*) *Student 2 should answer in the* negative, *and then ask if Student 1 has been to New York:* "No, I haven't; have you?" (Student 2 is also uncertain of Student 1's response.) *Student 1 answers in the* affirmative, *and tells when:* "Yes, I went last weekend." *Then the dialogue can continue in the simple past.*

*Student 2:* "What did you do? Where did you eat? When did you return?"

*Student 1:* "I saw the Statue of Liberty and I went to the Metropolitan Museum of Art and I ate hot dogs from a seller on the street. I came back on Friday."

We encourage our pairs in their role-plays to ask questions of their partners that the questioner truly doesn't know the answer to and we encourage them to improvise on topics that they are interested in.

Other possible starting questions include:

*Student 1:* Have you ever eaten octopus (*or something unusual*)? (*Student 2 must choose to a. answer in the positive present perfect and then use the simple past tense, or b. answer in the negative present perfect, with a corresponding question in the present perfect.*)

*Student 1:* Have you ever climbed a mountain (*something difficult*)? *Possible responses of Student 2 are*, "Yes, I climbed Mt. Fuji . . ." *or* "No, I haven't. Have you?"

This is not unlike hundreds of other grammar lessons we have done. Here is the added zest of the drama technique: Borrowing from Carolyn Graham's idea of jazz chants, or more recently rap songs, expands the grammar lesson into a choral chant. Divide the class into two sides. One side will be Student 1, chanting "Have you ever climbed a mountain?" over and over, to the rhythm you establish. The other side will be Student 2, chanting, "No, I haven't. Have you?" over and over when you direct them to respond. After each side has practiced questioning and answering, you can point first to Student 1 and then to Student 2 to make the chants into a conversation. Then you may introduce, "Yes, I climbed Mt. Fuji." You, the teacher, keep the rhythm going by pointing to the side you want to speak and giving them a cue word. You may then reverse the questioners and answerers, so that everyone gets a chance to practice asking and answering.

## Advanced Levels

At advanced levels, students feel that they should do more interacting with native speakers. For some students, this is a happy challenge; they are not discouraged when they make "mistakes." They keep trying and manage to work around any misunderstanding that occurs. On the other hand, we have seen students who begin to lose confidence at this critical point. When they are not understood, or are impatiently interrupted, they retreat from the front lines of interaction with native speakers and they lose enthusiasm for the new language. At this level, it is impossible for students to arm themselves with memorized conversations—interactions with native speakers are too unpredictable and complicated. But if we give them classes that compel them to use the language in a safe environment, that pull them into interactions with other class members, they will gain confidence to risk using the language outside the classroom.

We also like to use dramatic literature at advanced levels to introduce the great variety of forms the language uses to express emotions and ideas. There are some modes of expression that are almost never touched upon in a second language classroom, such as anger or great elation. But if a class enters into a piece of drama, to prepare it for performance, the students can explore how to say words in a more expressive way. At this point in the language learning curve, we want to encourage in-depth conversations on all kinds of topics. We want our students to think on their feet, so to speak, responding to unpredictable questions and answers from their classmates. Improvisations based on readings, like dramatizing a short story, or based on real-life problems of the students, like getting a parking ticket and arguing their way out of having to pay, or like simulating an exchange with a teacher about a late paper, are all helpful exercises and may help the students cope with life outside the second language classroom.

## The Best Environment for Speaking the Second Language

We feel that in drama and role-play classes students have the best chance to speak the second language at length (an explanation of what we mean by *drama* and *role play* is in the Introduction). We teachers can set up situations and we can fade into the background. Students speak many structures, familiar as well as new, in exercises and role-play and even memorized parts in a play. If the class' atmosphere is relaxed, they discover that they can make mistakes without losing face. If we give them a goal of performing for peers in our program, the actors aim at perfecting pronunciation because they know they have to communicate the ideas and emotions of a play with people who are seeing and hearing the work for the first time. In rehearsals we can tell them that no one will understand them the way they are saying a line. This is far more bluntly honest than we would be in a regular class. We can ask them to repeat over and over again an unintelligible word or phrase, to focus on improving pronunciation or phrasing *for realistic reasons.*

No matter what the level of your students is, it is a good idea to establish a few "rules" in the first few days. These rules are not hard and fast, but rather are designed to give students certain base expectations: the type of class, the need for cooperation, the evaluation procedures, and some of the signals they need to know in order that the class can move smoothly from exercise to exercise.

## Getting Started

In the following section of this chapter we shall set out how to organize a class that is dedicated wholly to drama and role-play. Whether the class lasts a week, a session of seven weeks, or a semester, the suggestions that we include here should help you set out the ground rules for a drama class but also allow you flexibility.

First, teachers should communicate that, although much of what is done in the class will seem like play, it is a serious class. Students will have fun, but they will work hard at using the language every day. Next, students must understand the directions and rules of the class. The teacher will be using gestures or short commands and the students must agree to do quickly what is being asked of them. Thirdly, this is an interactive class; they will be working in groups and it is essential that everyone participate. The overeager talkers must be quiet at times so that the very quiet members of the class feel that they have the opportunity to talk. Finally, cooperation is the key to the success of this kind of class.

### Setting the Atmosphere

Our first task is to set out clearly for the students what kind of a class this will be. We explain to the students that this class will probably be different from other classes: they will not be sitting at their desks; they will be moving around the room, listening to or giving directions, and they will be doing exercises without being able to refer to their books. We tell them that they will rarely be working alone: this is a class heavily dependent on group work and we expect them to harmoniously work together. At first, they may perceive the exercises as play and not serious language teaching, but we inform them that if they attend regularly and work very hard, they will eventually feel more comfortable in this new language.

We tell them that we do assign homework. We may ask them to analyze a character, to write a character biography, to keep a journal, to listen for and learn their cues, and to memorize lines. They will see that drama is connected to other aspects of language learning, such as reading in depth, writing, listening, mastering pronunciation, and acquiring vocabulary. We explain that if they do not do these homework assignments, their grades will be affected.

We explain that we evaluate them on such things as their regular attendance, their active participation, their cooperation in group work, their language improvement, and (if there is a play performed) their willingness to attend extra rehearsals and a final performance. We do not evaluate them as good or bad actors, but on their effort to improve in the language.

Neither teacher nor students can hide behind their books, never looking up, never making eye contact with another human being. At first some students may be nervous about giving up their books and paper and pencils. They may hang back and halfheartedly join in the exercises the first day, but if we are enthusiastic and join in the exercises with them, they usually will follow along. When we have encountered a reluctant student "actor," we proceed with optimistic caution. We don't insist or push people to do what they don't want to do. Each student is different and responds according to personality, and some may need longer to adjust to our methods. Rarely have we had a student who eventually did not cooperate. Teachers may want to consider having the students keep a journal (maybe on email) to record how they feel about the exercises they are asked to do. In this way the teacher has a finger on the pulse of the emotional reactions of the students and can change direction if it is obvious that the class as a whole is not responding in a favorable way to certain exercises.

Some teachers have told us that they cannot teach without seeing their lesson plan in front of them. For teachers who worry about this, we recommend using the overhead projector. They can list the day's activities for all to see. If they are concerned about giving up some of their authority, we remind them that the trade-off is students who use language actively, who are willing to take risks with language because they have been experimenting with it every day in class under a teacher's supervision.

In this chapter we include exercises that will help both you and your students lose some fears in working in this way. Certainly, in the first week or two, the exercises and games should be geared toward getting the students acquainted with each other and with you, their teacher. The goal is to create a nonthreatening atmosphere where the students can trust each other as they gain confidence in using the language and lose their fears about making mistakes.

## First-Week Exercises

### Introductions (formal)
Tell students a little bit about your background.

- Name and qualifications
- Why you are teaching this class
- What you hope to help students achieve
- If you have acted or directed before

Ask students what they expect from the class.

- Name and previous educational background
- Why did they take this class?
- What do they want (think is possible to achieve) by the end of the class?
- Have they ever acted before?

## Introductions: Alphabetical adjective game (informal)

Have the students volunteer as many adjectives as they can think of in three minutes.

- In groups—students work in small groups at the board, with one of them writing the adjectives on the board

or

- Whole class—teacher writes at the board as the class offers adjectives

Next, have the students choose adjectives from the list on the board or have them think of other adjectives not on the list that begin with the first letter of their given name (the name they wish to be called). For instance, Ardent Ann or Judicious Julie.

Then, have the students stand in a circle and ask them to introduce themselves in the following manner:
"My name is (*name*). I am called (*adjective*) + (*name*)."
When they are finished naming themselves, have them go around the room again, only this time they introduce the person next to them:
"The person next to me is (*name*). He/She is called (*adjective*) + (*name*)."

(*Tip*: It is a good idea to have at least one adjective in mind for each letter of the alphabet. A teacher once had a student whose name began with an *X* and when the student said he couldn't think of an adjective that began with that letter, she was unprepared to give him one.)

You may go around the room again having every student name all the students with their chosen adjectives, changing the exercise slightly to incorporate a different structure, and adding information about that student:

"I am Judicious Julie. I am from England. Ardent Ann is from America. Careful Claudia is from Argentina." And so on. (And, of course, the students love it when the teacher has to name them all.)

Sometimes we will repeat this exercise at the beginning of class for several days. Each time we do it, we add new information or change the structure. Possible additions: hobbies, last movie this person saw, favorite piece of music, favorite book, an animal that begins with the same first letter as your name, and so on. Different structures: "Ardent Ann adores anteaters." "Nervous Nadia never does needlework," and "Majestic Mario munches meatballs." (We always allow students to change the adjective if they so wish. Once, a friendly, bubbly Mia named herself Mad Mia and she did not want to be known as Mad Mia for the rest of the semester.)

## Introductions

Students pair off and introduce each other to the class after interviewing each other (if the class has an uneven number of students you may want to create one group of three).

- As a whole class, students decide on questions to ask. The teacher or designated student writes the questions on the board. Students copy questions on the left side of the paper, leaving room for the answers on the right side.
- In pairs, students interview each other, writing down the interviewee's answers.
- During the interviewing, the teacher writes on the board possible phrases used to introduce (such as, "Ann have you met Julie?") Use the following scenarios: 1. a young person to someone of the same age, 2. a young person to an older person, 3. a student to the president of the university.
- One by one, students introduce each other to the class.

## Survey: A good icebreaker

In this exercise, a list is distributed to each member of the class. The list includes phrases such as:

- Owns a car
- Has a cat
- Speaks German (or French)
- Plays soccer
- Has a younger brother
- Is the youngest in the family
- Likes to get up early in the morning

- Never eats breakfast
- Is a vegetarian
- Has read Dickens
- Has seen (movie title)
- Doesn't like classical (or rock) music

You can add whatever additional elements you would like to this list.

All students go around the room with the list in hand and find one person who can say yes for one item; they then write that person's name on the list opposite that item. They move on to the next item, until each blank has a different student's name. (They meet more students if each name can appear only once.)

## Setting Up Classroom Directions

Sometimes directions will need to be given to a student without interrupting an ongoing interchange. All (students and teacher) need to agree on what gestures will convey that information silently and efficiently. For instance, how will a director of a scene indicate that someone (on stage or off) should stop talking? Or how can a director indicate that an actor should speak louder without disrupting the rehearsal?

## Follow me (do what I do): Getting familiar with teacher directions

The teacher explains that the class is to watch very closely and imitate everything the teacher does. It might be wise to demonstrate with one student before you ask the whole class to follow your actions.

The teacher stands up; sits down; looks to the left; looks up; looks to the right; looks down; holds up right hand and makes a fist; points to the ceiling with index fingers of both hands; brings index finger of right hand to lips (*shhh* position); opens hands and puts them behind ears; makes a vertical circle with a hand (indicating need for speed); stretches hands far apart.

Divide the class into two groups. Have each group choose a leader. The groups will decide for themselves the gestures for the following situations:

- Stop talking
- Speak louder
- Speak softer
- Speak more slowly
- Speak faster
- Turn around
- Back up
- Come closer to the edge of the stage (or to the audience)
- Move closer to the actor you are talking to
- Repeat
- Not clear

After the groups decide, they can share their group's gestures with the class as a whole. The class should practice using all gestures and then decide which they prefer to use. The teacher, or whoever directs a scene, is then obligated to use these selected gestures to communicate these ideas for the rest of the semester.

To make sure that everyone is clear about each gesture and its meaning, the teacher can perform a gesture and the class can guess which action is called for.

## Directions using language: Follow me (do what I say)—more teacher directions

The teacher explains to the class that, in order to use the rehearsal time efficiently, everyone needs to be clear about what to do when they hear an oral direction. These commands will be used throughout the semester, not just this hour, day, or week.

- Form a circle so that everyone can see everyone else. (Circles work very well for most of our exercises.) The teacher asks students to listen very carefully. Students must do what the teacher *says* to do. They will hear the command, but will not see the teacher executing it. Students must decide what the actions should be.
- The teacher says: "Stand up," "look left," "sit down," "look at the ceiling," "stand up again," "walk to your left," "turn right," "turn around and face the person behind you," "breathe in," "take two steps and let your breath out," "breathe in again and, as you walk forward, say 'aaah,'" "when you are out of

15

breath, stand still," "bend over," "stand up straight again," "put your right hand over the head of the person nearest to you," "pick up your books," and whatever else you can devise to challenge the students to pay attention to what you say and to follow the directions easily. (Don't allow a lot of time for them to figure it out. You want them to respond quickly.)

## Alternatives

- Ask a student to call out the actions for the class to follow. That student may then ask some other student to issue the commands, and the second student may select another student to follow him or her.

- Or divide the class up into small groups and tell them that the leadership of the group will change when you whistle (or clap your hands); they should choose a "commander" to give the marching orders and the commanders must tell the group what to do. (It might be wise to suggest that they forget about ordering their group to leave the class—there's always some bright creative creature who would like to try the teacher's patience!)

- If it would make you feel more comfortable, you can control the commands by putting a list of them on the board. The students would not have to follow them in any particular order.

## What to Do When Problems Emerge?

First, we suggest that if you perceive that there is a problem, you try to get to the bottom of it immediately. Don't ignore it hoping that it will go away on its own. Small problems have a way of getting bigger if they aren't addressed right away. Types of problems include between students; teacher to student; cultural clashes within the class.

## Student to student

When we have had two students who are not getting along in our classes, we have used several tactics: talk with the students separately so that we understand each person's perspective; have the students talk to each other with the teacher acting as a mediator; ask the students if they would like to talk with someone outside the class about their problem; separate the students, assuming that you have more than one class at that level.

## Teacher to student

When we have had a student who was intentionally dominating the class, not allowing anyone else a chance to participate, we have taken that student aside after class hours and explained that that kind of behavior would not be tolerated. We tell them that we understand that they are eager to show what they have learned, but so are all the other students. We ask them to cooperate and allow others to speak. If the behavior persists, we have sometimes asked the student to be a group leader—to work with other students to get them to speak. Someone within that group is to keep track of the number of minutes that each of them speaks and if anyone dominates, that person has to be quiet during the next exercise.

## Cultural clashes

What do the students perceive as a problem? Once we had a class that was equally divided between Asian students and students from Latin America. Together we had read an essay that explained that in polite Asian society, it was common for people to wait until the speaking person stops before offering their opinions. This was a revelation to the Latin American students who talked whenever they perceived the least little pause (as we native English speakers frequently do). During the discussion of this reading, they listened as their Asian classmates finally admitted that they felt that they had been silenced by the constant interruptions of their Spanish-speaking classmates.

What could be possible solutions to the problem(s)? We asked the students how they felt. Both sets of students felt that just being aware of a cultural difference was an enormous step in the right direction.

In addition, we teachers offered language to defuse what might have been an explosive situation. (For instance, use *I* rather than *you*. Examples: "Excuse me, I would like to add my opinion." And, "Excuse me, may I speak now?" rather than "You never let me speak!")

The Asian students in that class learned to speak up with "I am not finished yet" rather than to sit quietly fuming at the perceived rudeness of the Spanish-speaking classmates. The Spanish-speaking students learned to ask, "May I speak now?"

## Role-play: A Follow-up to the Discussions over Problems

The teacher writes on the board phrases that can be used:

- Excuse me, I didn't understand. Could you please explain that?
- Excuse me, I think I disagree.
- Excuse me, I didn't hear you. Could you please repeat that?
- Excuse me, but I think that (*name*) wasn't finished speaking.
- Excuse me, I would like to finish my thought.
- May I add something?

The teacher divides the class into groups of three or four. In a small group each student may choose one of the following roles: one student who always enthusiastically interrupts; one student who is very quiet; one student who is a student leader, responsible for seeing that everyone talks; one student who is giving a talk (the student gets to choose the topic); or one student who constantly comments to a neighbor.

The teacher directs students to practice using these phrases in an imaginary situation where one student is annoying the others. Students may eventually write up their dialogues so that they can perform them in front of the whole class.

## Beginning Each Day

We find that it is a good idea to begin each class with a couple of warm-up exercises. Inasmuch as we do not like to work at our desks in this class and we may or may not be entering a classroom that is our own for all five hours of the intensive program day, we set up our physical space. We move the desks to the edges of the room, maybe while reciting some small thing that was part of the previous day's activities or repeating some nonsensical phrase, like "I push, she pulls." We might ask that our students move the desks in a particular manner, that is, slowly or speedily, or as a teenager who wishes to get the attention of someone of the opposite sex, or of someone who is trying to avoid being seen by a designated other person in the class, or as someone whose right foot is hurting, and so on. When the desks are out of the way, we form a circle. It is a good idea to do a few physical exercises, such as touch your toes or reach for the sky or twist to the right or left. (See Relaxation Exercises in Chapter 2.) As the students enter, you can assign someone to call out the exercises. Allow no more than five minutes for these setups. It is wise to specify to anyone who arranges room assignments for your program that you prefer a room that does not have fixed seating, that is, tables and chairs that are anchored to the floor.

Next, you may want to do a few vocal exercises, to work on particular sound combinations—for example: "Today's sound is *bl* as in blonde." We go around the circle and, face to face, watch how students form the sound and then demonstrate directly in front of each how we form that sound. The students sometimes laugh at our exaggerated demonstrations, but we are always amazed at how willingly they will attempt to conform to our examples. We usually don't have to ask students to continue to practice even if we have passed them in the circle; they just love the practice time and voluntarily continue on their own. (See Chapter 2 for more pronunciation exercises and vocal exercises.) After a few physical and vocal exercises, we are ready to start the rehearsal for the day.

## End of Class Wrap-up and Other Signals to Ward off Chaos

It is a good idea to set up for your class a signal for them to stop what they are doing. There may be times when they will be working in groups and you will need to get their attention. You might find it handy to flash lights or to have a little bell and when they notice the lights going on and off or hear that bell, they know that all action and vocalization should cease. In drama classes, where there may be three or four groups working at once, the noise level can be high; when the students are very focused in their own group, it may be difficult to get their attention. If you set forth a time or a signal when all activity is to halt, your students won't be able to get away with saying they didn't hear an announcement at the end of class because there was too much noise. They will know that at five minutes before the end of class or at the flashing of lights or the sound of the bell, they must be still and give the teacher full attention. Review what you have done and remind students what is to come.

You may set up your own segments of the class and your own rules that make the class more comfortable for you, but keep in mind what we said at the beginning of this chapter: your enthusiasm for what you do is very important. Be flexible and keep your students talking at the expense of your own precious pearls of wisdom. Join in with your students—this puts them at ease. And last, but certainly not least, we encourage you to set various goals for your classes. At beginning levels, these goals should be simple and practical. At higher levels, we think your students will thank you for giving them a goal of performing—whether for a public audience within the institute or just for other members of their class is not important. Literary texts by great playwrights will expand their vocabularies, and texts of their own making will make them search for ways of expressing ideas they are interested in. What is important is that you will have given them the opportunity to feel fluent, and that is very important indeed.

# Chapter Two

## Developing Fluency and Getting Students on Their Feet

In Chapter 1, we described how to get started in a drama class. In this chapter, we outline a number of exercises that enable students to work on various aspects of acting. In the exercises that follow, students stand up, move around the room, and experiment with how to use their voices, faces, and bodies when speaking a second language. A lot of the exercises can be used either as the focal point of a lesson or as a short practice prior to rehearsals. For exercises that require the use of a text, we illustrate the exercises using our skit *Nosey Busy Body* (Burke/O'Sullivan; see Appendix 2 for full script) as an example, but these exercises can easily be adapted to suit the text you are using with your class. Some of the exercises refer explicitly to English; if you are teaching a different language, the exercises will need to be adapted to suit that language.

We indicate the aim and length of each exercise as well as the preparation and procedure for each exercise. The time indicated is only a suggestion; you can adjust the time spent on each exercise according to how well it works with your students. The exercises are divided into the following categories:

- Relaxation exercises
- Voice exercises
- Pronunciation exercises
- Facial expression exercises
- Gesture exercises

21

- Posture exercises
- Movement exercises
- Mime exercises
- Improvisation exercises

# Relaxation Exercises

You might ask why we use relaxation exercises in a language class. These exercises help students become aware of the difference between relaxation and tension in each muscle in the body. Relaxation is the key to good acting. If students are relaxed, they are less self-conscious and more willing to experiment during rehearsals.

## Deep Breathing

**Aim:** Students become aware of how to use the breath to relax.
**Time:** 3 minutes
**Preparation:** None
**Procedure:** Ask students to close their eyes and breathe in and out normally. Then ask them to count silently and slowly to five with the next intake of air. Can they hold the breath for two counts? Next, ask them to breathe out slowly, silently counting to five or until they have expelled all air.

## Breathing with Vowels

**Aim:** Students warm up and relax the facial muscles.
**Time:** 3 minutes
**Preparation:** None
**Procedure:** While standing, students breathe in as deeply as they can, maybe even yawning once or twice. As they breathe out, they say the five vowels (a, e, i, o, u) running each vowel into the next one and holding the last one as long as possible. (When saying the vowel, there is tension in the facial muscles. When the students have finished the vowel sounds, they should relax the jaw muscles, letting the mouth drop open.)

## Tensing and Relaxing

**Aim:** Students learn to release tension from the muscles.

**Time:** 5 minutes

**Preparation:** None

**Procedure:** Students start in a standing position and then bend over as if to touch the toes. Students let the head and arms hang loosely in this position. They breathe normally. While breathing in slowly, students stand up one back bone at a time until they roll up to an upright position and then stretch their arms over their heads, which pulls them up onto their toes. With the expulsion of air, students slowly release the tension in their feet so that they are again flat on the floor, and in their arms, letting them fall to their sides. The students release the tension in their necks and let their backs begin to curl over until they are fully bent over again with arms hanging loosely from their sockets.

# Voice Exercises

In these exercises, students discuss how different voices sound and practice manipulating the voice to create different effects.

## Different Voices—A Cultural Perspective

**Aim:** To raise students' awareness about voices used in various countries and the impressions these voices make

**Time:** 20 minutes (10 minutes each day)

**Preparation:** None

**Procedure (first day):** Illustrate to your class a particular voice trait. For example, say a few sentences in a deep, booming voice or in a high-pitched, breathy voice. Ask the class what kind of person they think you are when you use that voice—for example, strong or weak, polite or impolite, intelligent or stupid (or a king, a president, a farmer, a beggar, a person of low or high class).

In pairs, preferably students from different cultures, students imitate the voice used by men and women in their own countries if a person is polite, impolite, intelligent, shy, cute, sexy, authoritative, weak.

**Homework:** Students choose a voice characteristic that is very common for men or women in their countries. For example, a student from Japan could speak in a high-pitched, breathy voice, which is a polite way for a Japanese woman to speak. They then interview three people, if possible, of different nationalities. They first demonstrate the voice characteristic, state whether it is a male or female voice, and ask the interviewee what kind of person has that voice.

**Procedure (second day):** In small groups, students discuss their findings from the homework interviews. Ask the whole class if one voice trait was perceived in different ways in different countries. Is a trait always perceived the same way in one country or are we just creating stereotypes?

## Different Voices—An American Perspective

**Aim:** Introducing students to different American voices

**Time:** 10 minutes

**Preparation:** Find some clips from movies or TV programs with exaggerated voice types in English—for example, Marilyn Monroe (soft, breathy, sexy voice); the Penguin from Batman (nasal, confident voice); Mafia voices (tough, deep, garbled); the voice of Uriah Heep from Charles Dickens' *David Copperfield* (smarmy, fawning); the modern businesswoman like Sigourney Weaver in the movie *Working Girl* (strong, deep, and confident).

**Procedure:** You can either let your students hear the sound without the picture or let them see the picture with the sound turned down.

## Procedure 1: Sound only

Turn the TV around or cover the screen so that the students hear only the sound. Play two or three video clips each with a different American voice. While listening, students should think about the following questions:

- What does the voice sound like? Describe it (for example: brassy, husky, guttural, strident, breathy, authoritative, nasal, or pinched).

24

- What do you expect when you hear this voice? What is the age, status, or occupation of the speaker?
- What impression does the person and the voice make on you? Positive or negative? Is this a strong or weak person, a shy or outgoing person?

The whole class discusses answers to the questions.

Play the clips again but this time let the students see the picture and hear the sound.

## Procedure 2: Picture only

Play the video clips to your students with the sound turned down. While watching the clips students should think about the following questions:

- What kind of voice does each person have?
- What kind of people can you see? Are they strong, weak, intelligent, or aggressive?
- Is voice production (high or low pitch, loud or soft dynamics) linked to personality or cultural expectations? What effect does career choice have on the voice? For example, does the president of a country usually talk with a regional accent?

As a whole class, discuss the students' answers to the questions.

Play the clips once again so that the students see the picture and hear the sound. Afterwards, discuss students' reactions. Did their perceptions about the people change once they had the visual and audio clues?

## Procedure 3: Jigsaw

For this exercise, you will need two rooms that each contain a TV, and two copies of the videotape.

Divide your class into two groups. One group watches the screen without sound in one room and the second group simultaneously listens to the sound without seeing the picture in the second room. Then, pair a student from group 1 with a student from group 2. They each describe the kind of person they saw or heard and with that information form a clearer picture of the people on the screen. Finally show the clips again with sound and vision to both groups. They can discuss whether their perceptions about the speakers changed after they saw and heard them.

## Loud and Soft Words

**Aim:** Students experiment with different facets of the voice.
**Time:** 5 minutes
**Preparation:** None
**Procedure:** Choose any word—for example, *ice* or *hello*. You and your students stand in a circle and say the word in unison. Every-one starts very quietly and gradually gets louder and louder, then gradually softer and softer. The student on the teacher's left says the word softly; the student on the left of that student says the word loudly, and so on around the circle. Next, have one student in the circle say the word in a very low-pitched voice, each student in turn then says the word in a slightly higher-pitched voice than the previous student. Your students can also say the word conveying different emotions when you give verbal cues—for example, hap-pily, angrily, sadly, defiantly (you may need to go over the ad-verbs before class to make sure the students understand your instructions).

## Projecting the Voice

**Aim:** To teach students how to use the breath and abdomen when saying lines
**Time:** 5 minutes
**Preparation:** None
**Procedure:** The whole class stands in a circle. Students stand up straight with their shoulders back, heads up looking straight ahead. Tell them to relax their shoulders and place their hands on their sides with their thumbs to the back and their fingers spread out from the lower rib down to the waist. You may need to go around to help them with this. Students should breathe in deeply not al-lowing their chests or shoulders to rise. Tell them they should be able to feel the ribs and abdomen expand outwards as they breathe in slowly and deeply.

Students breathe in deeply once again and as they breathe out slowly, they say the word *who* until they have no more air left (*whoooooooooooooooooo*).

Next, students stand in a line facing the teacher. They breathe in deeply again and when they breathe out, they say the word *who*, but this time very quickly and explosively using their stomach muscles to push the breath out of their abdomens.

Give your students a line from the text you are using and ask them to say it by breathing deeply into the abdomen and pushing the words out from the abdomen as they breathe out. Each time the students say the line, you take a step back and tell them they have to say the line so that you can hear it. Use a gesture to indicate if they need to lower their voices (point downwards) or if the volume is not okay (hand behind ear). Continue in the same way and step farther and farther away from the students so that they have to project their voices more each time. Remind them that they should use their abdomen muscles to push the words out whenever they breathe out.

## Nonsense Conversation

**Aim:** Students explore the rhythms and music of English phrases and sentences through nonsense sounds.
**Time:** 20 minutes
**Preparation:** None
**Procedure:** Stand in front of the class and greet your students, but instead of using words say, "Blah blah blah," and use pitch, volume, stress, rhythm, and intonation to create meaning. It is very important in this exercise that neither you nor your students use gestures; meaning should be created only through the voice. Say, "Blah blah" so that it sounds like "Hello." Next, say, "Blah blah blah" in imitation of "How are you?" Ask students what they think you were saying to them. Next, students work in pairs and, in turn, ask a question, give a command, and make a statement in English using "Blah blah blah" (remind them that they are not to use any gestures). Then ask volunteers to demonstrate a question, command, and statement to the class saying only, "Blah blah blah." Ask the whole class the following questions about the question, command, and statement:

- How do the question, command, and statement sound different?
- Are there differences in pitch, stress, rhythm, intonation or volume? If so, try to describe the differences and when they occur.

In pairs, students have conversations using "Blah blah blah" using the following contexts. Give a short example of the first context to get students started. Give students a few minutes to go through each of the situations.

- A is trying to convince B of something, but B is not convinced.
- B is trying to convince A of something and A is eventually convinced.
- A has had a fight with his or her girlfriend or boyfriend; B is a good friend who is trying to comfort A.
- B is trying to ask A out on a date; A is not interested.
- A is trying to ask B out on a date; B is interested.

When students have worked through all the contexts, volunteers demonstrate each of the situations.

## Nonsense Emotions

**Aim:** Students explore the sound of the voice when showing emotion.
**Time:** 15 minutes
**Preparation:** None
**Procedure:** The whole class lists a number of emotions that are written on the blackboard by a volunteer (for example, anger, disappointment, shock, hurt, triumph, sadness, fear, euphoria, guilt, pride, conceit, embarrassment, suspicion, nervousness, worry, empathy, surprise, compassion, relief, amusement). Choose one of the emotions—for example, anger—and ask students how they would depict that emotion using the voice. For example, when a person is angry, is the voice loud and maybe a bit shaky? Will the speaker speak fast with a lot of changes in intonation because of strong emotion? Suggest that they think about intonation, speed

28

of delivery, volume, and tone. Tell students you are going to show them anger by saying only "Blah blah blah." The situation is that "My friend borrowed my CD player, but she has broken it. I am very angry with her." Demonstrate this conversation to the students using "Blah blah blah." Then ask your students if there is another way to show anger in the voice.

In pairs, students choose one of the emotions on the blackboard and design a situation that demonstrates this emotion. After practicing the situation using "Blah blah blah," students demonstrate their conversations to the rest of their classmates, who guess which emotion is being illustrated.

## Voices of Characters

**Aim:** Students work on the voices of characters from a play.
**Time:** 10 minutes
**Preparation:** None
**Procedure:** Students working in pairs choose two characters from a play that the class has recently read. The pairs may work with any two characters from the play. They should decide on each character's voice in the following terms: pitch, volume, speed. Ask pairs to develop a situation (not one from the play) in which the characters they have chosen may improvise a dialogue; they should change the names of the characters. Have them write the situation on the board—for example, "Character 1 asks about a borrowed item; Character 2 reacts." They then act out the situation, using the voices they chose, for their classmates who must guess which characters are being portrayed.

## Emotions of Characters in a Text

**Aim:** Students identify emotions in a text and try to portray them when reading the lines.
**Time:** 15 minutes
**Preparation:** Students need to have read the text before doing this exercise. (For this exercise, you can either have all pairs work on the same passage or give each pair a different passage.)
**Procedure:** Students look at the following lines from *Nosey Busy*

*Body* (see Appendix 2), or lines from a text they are working with in class, and use them in the exercise below:

*Lines 28–31*

A: Do you know more about this than you're telling me?

B: Don't be ridiculous!

A: (*On the attack now*) You look guilty. Why are you blushing?

B: I'm not blushing! You're imagining things. I'm just warm. Isn't it warm in here? I'll open a window! (*Jumps up and goes to the window.*)

In pairs or small groups, students go over the text line by line and decide which emotions are being expressed by the characters. It will help your students if they write the emotions beside the relevant words. For example:

A: Do you know more about this than you're telling me? [*suspicious*]

B: Don't be ridiculous! [*nervous*]

Next, students discuss how to say the lines evoking the right emotions. Encourage them to write their ideas down on the text. For example:

A: Do you know more about this than you're telling me? [*suspicious*] [*should be said slowly, deliberately, with stress on* more]

B: Don't be ridiculous! [*nervous*] [*should speak fast; voice is high-pitched, breathless*]

Students practice saying the lines and then act them out for the class. The audience should decide whether the emotions were convincing. If the actors were unsuccessful, their classmates should suggest other ways of reading the lines in terms of speed, pitch, or volume. Even if all the students work on the same passage, there will surely be differences. Ask various students to speed up the delivery of a line or to slow it down and then ask the audience how the change affects meaning.

# Pronunciation Exercises

If students are going to dramatize a text and perform it for an audience, it is imperative that they work carefully on saying their lines. Before memorizing lines, students need to work intensively on stress, rhythm, intonation, and maybe the pronunciation of individual consonants and vowels. We suggest students focus particularly on prosody (stress, rhythm, and intonation), but if a student's pronunciation of a specific consonant or vowel is likely to hinder the audience's comprehension of what is happening in the play, work one-on-one with that student to overcome this problem.

## *Introduction to Stress, Rhythm, and Intonation*

**Aim:** Students start working on stress, rhythm, and intonation using a text.

**Time:** 30 minutes (approximately)

**Preparation:** Make one copy of the text for each student. We suggest you use jazz chants, poems for two voices, or limericks (see pronunciation books in Bibliography) because they have definite beats that can be clapped to or marched to.

**Procedure:** Give each student a copy of the same text and divide the class into two groups. Each group reads one part of the text: with jazz chants, each group takes one voice in the chant; with poems for two voices, each group reads one of the voices; with limericks, each group reads alternate lines.

Next, divide the class into pairs. They work with the same text and each partner takes one of the voices (jazz chants and poems for two voices) or read alternate lines (limericks). This time, they should say the words in many different ways—for example, putting the stress on different words, varying the intonation patterns, or using different rhythm (such as in the style of a rap song). Once they have found a version they like, they perform it for the class. After the performance, the whole class can discuss how different stress, rhythm, or intonation patterns can affect the meaning of the same words. Actors have the freedom to experiment in this way when rehearsing their lines.

## *Working with Lines from a Play*

Students can use the methods in the first pronunciation exercise to practice saying their lines from a play. This is the first step in the process. Students will continue to work on stress, rhythm, and intonation throughout rehearsals.

## *Working with Problematic Consonants and Vowels*

As mentioned earlier, if a student's pronunciation of a specific consonant renders a word, phrase, or sentence incomprehensible, they need some individual pronunciation coaching. We suggest you refer to some of the pronunciation books in the Bibliography for information about how consonants are produced and for minimal pair exercises. When working one-on-one with a student, proceed in the following manner:

- Sit very close and tell the student to watch your mouth very closely when you say the consonant or word.
- Explain how to pronounce the consonant physically and repeat the consonant a number of times.
- Encourage the student to repeat the consonant after you.
- Repeat a number of times (ten or more) the word from the student's lines containing the consonant, and then the student repeats it after you.
- Say the phrase containing the word many times and have the student repeat it after you.
- Say the whole sentence containing the word and have the student repeat it after you.

## Facial Expressions Exercises

Why use facial expressions exercises in a language class? Communication not only consists of speaking and pronunciation, but also body language: facial expressions, gestures, posture, and movement. These areas of communication are often left out of language classes (most textbooks in second language learning do not cover them) or only touched on in a pronunciation class if there is enough time. There is plenty of opportunity to experiment with appropriate facial expressions if you are rehearsing a play.

## Introduction

**Aim:** To introduce students to making facial expressions
**Time:** 5 minutes
**Preparation:** None
**Procedure:** Students make the following facial expressions on your oral cues (if they get stuck, illustrate the facial expression to them so they can copy it).

- Frown
- Raise both eyebrows/raise one eyebrow
- Twist your mouth
- Purse your lips
- Close your eyes
- Open your eyes very wide
- Wink
- Smile out of the side of your mouth
- Rapidly blink your eyes
- Smile sweetly
- Smile sarcastically
- Grit your teeth
- Wrinkle your nose

## Emotions in the Face

**Aim:** Students explore how to show emotion with their faces.
**Time:** 10 minutes
**Preparation:** Find three clips from movies or TV that show three different emotions depicted in the face—for example, anger, sadness, and fear. Ask students to bring a mirror to class if they have one and bring a few to class yourself if you have them.
**Procedure:** Ask students to look angry. Show students three different clips showing anger, sadness, and fear (or whichever emotions you were able to find). After each clip, ask students how the actor depicted the emotion using the face. Then, ask students to

copy what the actors did while looking in the mirrors to check their faces.

## Emotions Game

**Aim:** Students practice showing emotions with their faces.
**Time:** 10–15 minutes depending on the size of your class or the length of time you run the game
**Preparation:** Before class, write a number of emotions on separate pieces of paper and put them into an envelope (see the voice exercise "Nonsense Emotions" for a list of emotions).
**Procedure:** In turn, students come to the front of the class and choose a piece of paper with an emotion on it. They should quickly choose a facial expression to match the emotion and show it to the class. The class must guess which emotion the student is illustrating. (This could also be played as a team game. The students are put into two teams, A and B. A member of Team A takes a piece of paper with an emotion written on it out of the envelope at the front of the class. This student makes a face to portray the emotion and Team A tries to guess the emotion. If they guess correctly, they get two points. If they cannot guess, Team B may guess for one bonus point, if they are correct. The same procedure is followed for Team B and so on until everyone has had a turn.)

## Facial Expressions in a Text

**Aim:** Students decide on facial expressions to go with lines in a play.
**Time:** 10 minutes
**Preparation:** Students need to have read the text before class.
**Procedure:** In pairs, students work with a few lines of the play they are using in class. Students first decide how the characters feel when they say the lines and then choose suitable facial expressions to depict those feelings. After practicing for a few minutes, students join another pair and read their lines using the facial expressions. The pairs give each other feedback on how convincing the facial expressions are with the lines they say. Here are some

lines from *Nosey Busy Body*, which could be used for this exercise (some facial expressions have been added in square brackets as examples):

*Lines 8 and 9*

A: *(Deciding to take a chance)* [*biting lip*] Have you noticed anything about Elliott lately?

B: No. *(A little worried)* [*eyes look down*] What could I have noticed?

*Lines 15 and 16*

B: *(A little relieved)* *(Sits down)* No! There's nothing to worry about. [*false smile, tense face*] He's such a good guy. So loyal, so trustworthy.

A: *(A little suspicious)* [*looking out of the corner of the eye*] How can *you* be so sure?

*Line 24*

A: What are you laughing at?

*Line 30*

A: *(On the attack now)* [*glaring*] You look guilty. [*frowning*] Why are you blushing?

*Line 34*

A: *(Shocked)* [*mouth hangs open and gasps for air*] What kind of problems?

*Line 39*

B: No, I'm not. [*grimace*] Well, yes, I am. I have to call Ellio— [*mouth open in shock*] oh-oh—I mean Richard. [*frown*] I mean I've got to leave...

## Gestures Exercises.

Gestures are motions of the body or a part of the body to express or emphasize ideas and emotions.

### Introduction to Gestures

**Aim:** To introduce students to gestures and their meanings

**Time:** 10–15 minutes
**Preparation:** None
**Procedure:** Stand in front of the class and demonstrate to your students each of the gestures below. Students copy each gesture, then as a whole class discuss what the gesture means:

- Snapping fingers
- Drumming fingers on a table
- Stroking the chin
- Running fingers through the hair
- Tossing the head
- Lowering the eyes
- Hands on hips
- Arms crossed
- Hands clenched
- Hand on the cheek
- Hands in pockets
- Wringing your hands
- Pointing your finger
- Shaking your finger at someone
- Head in hands
- Arms outstretched (as if to embrace)
- Arms straight out in front with the palms up (meaning stay away)
- Shrugging shoulders

Ask students the following:

How do you show:
- That you are thinking?
- That you need more time?
- That you don't want to see this person?
- That somebody has done good work?
- That you dismiss someone from your presence?
- That you suspect that someone is watching/following you?

For homework, students either observe people or note what gestures they use to show the emotions in the following list, or students ask someone to show them what they do when they feel the following emotions:

- Anger
- Worry
- Suspicion
- Relief
- Excitement
- Fear
- Impatience

## Emotions in Gestures

**Aim:** Students discuss how people show emotions through gestures.
**Time:** 15 minutes
**Preparation:** Students need to have done the homework exercise in the first gestures exercise, "Introduction to Gestures."
**Procedure:** Students get into small groups and share what they observed or found out from the homework (see "Introduction to Gestures" exercise). Students get into pairs and choose an emotion. They should then decide on a situation for two people where one or both of the characters feel that emotion. Next they decide on gestures that best illustrate their chosen emotion. They practice their situation using words and gestures. Finally, they act out the situation for their classmates who guess which emotion is being portrayed.

## Gestures in a Text

**Aim:** Students decide on gestures to go with lines in a text.
**Time:** 10 minutes
**Preparation:** Students need to have read the text before class.
**Procedure:** In pairs, students work with a few lines of the play they are using in class. Students first decide how the characters feel when they say the lines and then choose suitable gestures to depict those feelings. After practicing for a few minutes, students join another pair and read their lines using the gestures. The pairs give feedback on how convincing the gestures are with the lines.

## Posture Exercises

Postures, like gestures, give clues to emotions and thoughts. Postures are body postures—for example: standing upright or bending over.

### *Introduction to Postures*

**Aim:** Students imitate postures and analyze the meaning.
**Time:** 10 minutes
**Preparation:** None
**Procedure:** Demonstrate the following postures to your students. After each one, ask students to imitate you and to decide what impression each posture makes. We have done the first one as an example:

- Slump down in a chair with feet on the table
  Impression: bored or lazy person with no respect for furniture or other people in the room.
- Sit upright behind a desk, very alert and nervous.
- Sit with arms folded, looking bored.
- Stand up very straight and look serious.
- Sit in a confident, relaxed manner.
- Sit slightly forward, frown, and point your finger at your students.
- Sit with arms folded, smiling.
- Lean back in the chair, arms folded, eyes closed.
- Lean forward in the chair, frown, and look serious.
- Place hands on hips (arms akimbo).

### *Different People, Different Postures*

**Aim:** Students assume postures of different kinds of people.
**Time:** 10–15 minutes
**Preparation:** Move tables to the edge of the room and make a large circle of chairs.
**Procedure:** Tell students they have to use their whole bodies to be different people. Divide the class into an equal number of A's and B's. Students respond to your oral cues:

- A's and B's are professors.
    1. Stand together.
    2. Sit together.
    3. Walk together.

- A's are professors and B's are students.
    1. Stand together.
    2. Sit together.
    3. Walk together.

- A's and B's are janitors.
    1. Stand together.
    2. Sit together.
    3. Walk together.

- A's are janitors and B's are bosses.
    1. Stand together.
    2. Sit together.
    3. Walk together.

- A's are husbands and B's are wives. Stand opposite each other:

    You have a good relationship.

    You have a bad relationship.

    You feel indifferent about each other.

    You are rich.

    You are poor.

    You are arguing over money.

    You are divorced.

## Postures of Characters in a Text

**Aim:** Students adopt the postures of characters from a text.
**Time:** 5 minutes

**Preparation:** Students need to be familiar with the characters from the text.

**Procedure:** Choose two characters from a text that students have read in class. Half of the class is Character 1; the other half is Character 2. Tell students to use their whole bodies to be the character during this exercise. Give students oral cues [we have used actions from *Nosey Busy Body* (see Appendix 2); you can use actions from the text that you are using in class in which two characters appear]:

- Walk around the room.
- Sit down.
- Stand up suddenly.
- Walk around nervously.
- Look at your watch.

## Postures in a Text

**Aim:** Students choose postures for particular lines in a text.

**Time:** Depends on how much text students work with.

**Preparation:** Students need to have read the text before the class.

**Procedure:** Students work in pairs with a text they are familiar with. They work line by line and describe characters' postures for each line. They should write their ideas next to the lines. Here are a few lines from *Nosey Busy Body* (see Appendix 2) that have been edited as an example:

*Lines 37–38*

B: [*Pacing up and down nervously*][*A sits upright rigidly and watches B carefully and suspiciously*] Well, you know, this [*stops and looks at watch*], um [*looks at watch*], client [*paces up and down again*] knows Richard and well, [*stops and faces A, appearing more confident*] obviously he thought he could help if he told Richard and then Richard told me because, [*looks at watch*] because . . .

A: [*Sitting very rigid and very agitated*] What's the matter with you? You're fumbling; you're hiding something! [*Stands up suddenly with hands on hips*] And why do you keep looking at your watch?

# Movement Exercises

In order to make a performance more interesting to watch and to appear more realistic, actors move around on stage. Movement on stage needs to look natural, but students feel self-conscious moving around at first, so they need to practice.

## *Walking Randomly*

**Aim:** Helps students relax and clear their minds at the beginning of class

**Time:** 3 minutes

**Preparation:** Move the desks, if you can, to the edges of the room.

**Procedure:** Students walk around the room in whichever direction they like. Tell them to change the speed when they hear your oral cues—for example, "fast," "slow," "normal speed," "stroll." They must not speak and they should avoid physical contact with classmates.

## *Walking Through Different Types of Terrain*

**Aim:** Students practice walking in different ways. It helps them to develop mime and movement skills.

**Time:** 5 minutes

**Preparation:** Move the desks to the edges of the room.

**Procedure:** Divide the class into two groups, A and B. First, everyone walks around the room as in the first movement exercise, "Walking Randomly." At your signal, A students freeze and B students walk as if they are in a very cold, snowy landscape. Next, B students freeze and A students walk as if they are in a very hot desert. Then, A students freeze and B students walk as if they are in a swamp.

## *Showing Emotions*

**Aim:** Students depict emotions using their bodies.

**Time:** 3 minutes

**Preparation:** Students need to know the emotions you use in this exercise.

**Procedure:** Students walk around the room. The teacher calls out an emotion and the students show this emotion while they walk. Give students about four or five emotions in turn—for example, anger, happiness, nervousness, sadness, fear.

## Sculptor and Sculpture

**Aim:** Students learn concentration and coordination.
**Time:** 10 minutes
**Preparation:** None
**Procedure:** In pairs, one student is the sculptor and the other a lump of clay. The sculptor tells the partner to move the body— for example, "Touch your shoulder with your right hand and stand on your left leg." The sculptor continues this until the lump of clay has become a sculpture. Once the sculptors in the room are satisfied with their creations, the statues must stand perfectly still and quiet holding the pose while the sculptors view the art exhibit and choose their favorite sculpture. Pairs then swap roles.

## Mirroring

**Aim:** Students learn concentration and how to move in sequence with other people (important for dramatic work).
**Time:** 5 minutes
**Preparation:** None
**Procedure:** In pairs, students face each other. Without speaking, one student starts to move slowly and the other student must copy this movement to create a mirror image. Students should take turns in leading and following each other.

## Observing Movement

**Aim:** Observing people's movements in everyday situations
**Time:** 15–20 minutes
**Preparation:** This is a homework exercise.
**Procedure:** As homework, students go to a public place—for example, a cafe, a store, or a park. They sit and observe one or two different people for about fifteen to twenty minutes, for example, they might watch a young child playing in the playground or an

old man walking his dog. They should observe that person's posture and movements. For instance, is the person standing upright in a confident manner or bent over? Is the person running around energetically, or walking very slowly with difficulty?

In class, students work in small groups and show the movements they saw to their classmates who try to guess what kind of person is being imitated.

## Personal Space

**Aim:** Students learn about people's personal space.
**Time:** 5 minutes
**Preparation:** None
**Procedure:** Ask two students to come to the front of the class and stand opposite each other. Tell one of the students to stand as close as they comfortably can to the person opposite. Ask the other student if that is okay. Then get the first student to step closer and see what the reaction of both students is. It is fun to have students of different nationalities do this, as the class will see the differences in personal space. You could actually measure the distance between different students with a tape measure to see which nationalities stand very close together and which don't.

Afterwards, discuss with the students what they noticed during this exercise. Which people felt comfortable standing close together? Was this because of nationality, familiarity, gender, status, or something else?

## Personal Space in Everyday Situations

**Aim:** Students observe people's personal space in everyday situations
**Time:** 10–15 minutes
**Preparation:** This is a homework assignment.
**Procedure:** As homework, students should go to a public place and observe how close people stand or sit for about ten to fifteen minutes. Students make notes about what they observe and try to determine why people are close or far away (age, gender, nationality). In class, they report their observations to their classmates.

## *Movements of Characters in a Text*

**Aim:** Students map out characters' movements in a text.

**Time:** Depends on the length of the text segment

**Preparation:** Students need to have read the text before class.

**Procedure:** Divide the class into small groups and give each group a section of the skit *Nosey Busy Body* (see Appendix 2), or lines from the text you are using in class. Each group, after reading the section a number of times, tries to visualize the movements or lack of movement that the characters make in each line of the text. Students can also think about physical distance between characters in this exercise. As the students decide on the movements, they write them down in the text. Students then say the lines while trying out the movements they chose. In groups of three or more, two students can read the lines while the third watches and evaluates the movements. Then they discuss what works with the text.

Finally, students act out their sections of text for the class who afterwards can make suggestions regarding the physical distance and movements of characters.

# Mime Exercises:
## Working With Objects That Are Not There

Mime is using only the actor's body and imagination to help the audience "see" what the actor sees. Two people sit at a table. They suggest by their movements where they are. If they pick up an imaginary cup of coffee and they pretend to have a conversation by nodding their heads and moving their lips noiselessly, they convey to the audience that they are in a café. To help the audience further understand the setting, one of them beckons to a waiter who goes to the table and mimes taking orders. In the exercises that follow students create situations without using their voices.

## *Telephoning*

**Aim:** Students practice postures, facial expressions, and gestures in situations on the telephone.

**Time:** 5–10 minutes

**Preparation:** Write the situations on the blackboard.

**Procedure:** Students mime the following situations while on the telephone:

- You call a pizzeria and ask for a pizza without anchovies; obviously the answerer doesn't understand.
- You call your parents and ask for money; obviously your father surprises you and . . .
- You call your girlfriend/boyfriend, but a strange man/woman answers the telephone.

After students have practiced alone, ask a few of them to demonstrate the three situations.

## Actions in Detail

**Aim:** Students use their imaginations and have to help an audience easily understand what they are doing.

**Time:** 10–15 minutes

**Preparation:** None

**Procedure:** Tell students that often actors have to mime when acting. Therefore, they should depict movements for a scene in as much detail as possible to help the audience understand what the actor is doing. In pairs, students choose an everyday action—for example, unpacking the shopping, cleaning the apartment, watching TV, or unwrapping a present. They first discuss the action in as much detail as they can and then mime it, showing as much of this detail as possible to make the audience imagine where they are and what they are doing. For example, they could mime unpacking their groceries, where they would need to take the purchased items from the grocery bags to the cupboard or fridge. They would need to show the shape of each object and carry it to the appropriate place, maybe drop something (a carton of milk) and have to wipe the floor clean. Maybe one of them bought something that she shouldn't have and the other unpacks it from the bag. After practicing, each pair demonstrates the mime to the classmates who have to guess what is happening.

## Driven to Distraction

**Aim:** Students have to concentrate very hard despite obvious distraction.

**Time:** 5 minutes

**Preparation:** None

**Procedure:** Students work in pairs. One student mimes a very simple action and repeats it over and over again—for example, putting a letter in an envelope, writing the address on the front, and placing a stamp on it. Another situation could be a famous person being hounded by a newspaper photographer. The student's partner tries as hard as possible to distract the student from miming that action. The distracter is allowed to talk but not touch. After about two minutes, tell the students to swap roles.

## Actions Game

**Aim:** Students use all their powers of imagination to convey actions to their team members.

**Time:** 15–20 minutes depending on the size of the class

**Preparation:** None

**Procedure:** Divide the class into two teams. Each team makes a list of actions and does not let the other team know what they have written. Encourage the students to make the actions challenging— for example, trying to get off a crowded bus and missing your stop. Then, Team B chooses one action from their list and shows it to a student from Team A. That student must mime the action to Team A. If Team A guesses within thirty seconds, they get two points; if they guess within one minute, they get one point. Then Team A gives an action to a member of Team B who mimes that action for Team B and so on. You can modify the game by using famous people or places instead of actions. This game is always fun if students give each other difficult mimes.

# Improvisation Exercises

## Talking for One Minute

**Aim:** This is a good exercise to develop concentration when performing to an audience.

**Time:** 5–10 minutes
**Preparation:** Write topics on small pieces of paper before class—for example, favorite dessert, James Bond, a funny experience, your earliest memories.
**Procedure:** Students are given a topic and have to speak in front of the whole class nonstop for one whole minute without hesitating or laughing; it does not matter what they say as long as they begin on topic and talk continuously. If you have a large group, divide the class into smaller groups.

## Verbal Boxing (a Concentration Exercise)

**Aim:** Students have to talk without being distracted by what their partner is saying.
**Time:** 5 minutes
**Preparation:** Write topics on pieces of paper (see the first improvisation exercise for some examples of topics you could use).
**Procedure:** In pairs, students choose one topic. They face each other and both talk on the same topic at the same time. The idea is to keep talking without hesitating or laughing. The person who can outtalk the other is the winner. Hilarious, but very difficult!

## Retelling a Story

**Aim:** Students dramatically tell a famous story using some object that is readily available.
**Time:** 10 minutes
**Preparation:** Choose a story that everyone in the class knows.
**Procedure:** As a whole class, summarize the story. The students then put only one object on their desks (a hat, a pencil, a bar of chocolate, anything is fine). In turn, students dramatically retell a small part of the story using their own objects. For example, if the story is *Cinderella* and a student has a key, the student could state that the ugly stepsisters locked Cinderella in the kitchen and threw away the key. Students must continue telling the story from the point at which the previous person stopped and include the objects on their own desks. Tell students that they can change the original story in any way they like.

## News Anchor (a Concentration Exercise)

**Aim:** Students are put in an awkward situation where they must read prepared lines at the front of the room while others are trying to distract them. This is a great exercise in concentration and provides exposure to what it is like being on stage.

**Time:** 25 minutes

**Preparation:** Students and the teacher each read an article for homework and summarize it in writing in three to five sentences. They should practice saying these sentences in a formal and clear way and bring the summary to class.

**Procedure:** Start the class by discussing what a TV news anchor is like: formal manner, clear voice, upright body stance, and so on. Tell students that together you are all going to create a TV news program in the classroom. The desk and chair at the front of the room represent the TV studio and the space in front of the desk and chair represents someone's home. Tell students that when they are sitting behind the desk, they are in a TV studio and cannot see what is happening in the rest of the classroom. When they are not sitting behind the desk, students are all in someone's living room watching a news program together. They should do whatever they usually do while watching TV—for example, comment on what they are watching, have conversations amongst themselves, leave the room and come back, talk on the telephone, turn the volume up and down.

To get used to the feeling of being behind the desk, students, in turn, sit behind the desk, greet the rest of the class, say their names, and then say goodbye in the manner of a news anchor.

Next, discuss the format of a TV news program. For example, the anchor in the studio begins and often passes the story over to another correspondent in a different place. Ask students how links are made between the different people. How does the TV news program begin and how does it end? What phrases are used? For example: "Now, we'll go to our correspondent in Tokyo for more details."

When you are all ready, the TV program begins. Students take turns to come up and sit behind the desk and read their sentences as if they are items in a news program. They should concentrate on looking at the camera and saying their sentences clearly, while ignoring everything that their classmates are doing.

When students are finished reading, they have to create a link to the next person.

The other students act like they are sitting in their living room at home and do whatever they like. Students really enjoy trying to distract the news anchors. However, the news anchors should do their best not to be distracted by the other students. We join in the exercise and also try as hard as possible to distract the news anchor. When it is the teacher's turn, usually last, the students have a great time getting their revenge!

## *I'm Sorry!*

**Aim:** Students improvise a situation based on an apology.
**Time:** 20 minutes
**Preparation:** Write the following on separate cards:

1A: Child
1B: Parent
2A: Mechanic
2B: Car owner
3A: Husband
3B: Wife
4A: President
4B: Journalist
5A: Roommate
5B: Roommate
6A: Boss
6B: Worker
7A: Worker
7B: Boss
8A: Gangster
8B: Gangster boss

**Procedure:** Put students in pairs and give each student a card: A or B. For example, the first pair get cards 1A and 1B, the second pair 2A and 2B and so on. Tell them A will apologize to B. To-gether, they need to decide on a context for the apology: Why is A apologizing to B? Is A sincere about the apology? Does B accept the apology?

After discussing the situation, students can work on the dia-logue. However, there are some restrictions:

- There should only be two exchanges, A B A B or B-A-B-A.
- A can only say, "I'm sorry."

For example, if you use role cards 1A: Child and 1B: Parent, you might have this dialogue:

*A:* I'm sorry.

*B:* It's all very well apologizing now, but you shouldn't have given the key to your little sister.

*A:* I'm sorry.

*B:* Now we've got two problems: the key is in your sister's stom-ach and we are locked outside!

Students practice the dialogue and then present the dialogue to their classmates who guess who the two characters are and what the context is.

## Different Contexts, Same Story

**Aim:** Each student takes on a role and presents it to the class.
**Time:** 15 minutes
**Preparation:** Write the dialogue on the board before class.
**Procedure:** In pairs, students work on the dialogue below. They decide who the two characters are and where the dialogue takes place. For example, Person A is romantically interested in B. B is not at all interested in A. A knows that B usually goes jogging in the park, so A accidentally on purpose is also jogging at the same time as B. After students have practiced the dialogue, they present it to the class; their classmates guess who the two characters are. We have used this exercise many times and every time students come up with very original situations. There are endless possibilities.

*Person A:* How are you?

*Person B:* Fine.

*Person A:* Do you want to go for a coffee?

*Person B:* I can't, I'm busy.

*Person A:* Oh, bye then.

*Person B*: Bye.

## Telephone Conversation

**Aim:** Students improvise a situation on the telephone.

**Time:** 5–10 minutes

**Preparation:** None

**Procedure:** Put students into groups of three. Each member of a group should sit close to each other in a circle, but facing away. Give each student a number. Tell them the following situation:

> Student 1 and Student 2 are having a telephone conversation (you can decide who you are and what your relationship is before starting the improvisation).
>
> During your conversation Student 3 comes into the conversation. You have a crossed line. What do you do?
>
> What is the reaction of Students 1 and 2?
>
> How does the situation develop?
>
> Does Student 3 leave the line?

After students have finished their improvisations, ask each group to report what happened during the telephone conversation.

## One-liners

**Aim:** Students improvise a conversation based on one line of dialogue.

**Time:** 15 minutes

**Preparation:** Write the sentences on separate pieces of paper.

**Procedure:** Divide the class into pairs and either give all pairs the same sentence or each pair a different sentence. Students discuss the sentence and come up with a dialogue that begins with that sentence. After they have practiced the dialogue, they present it to the class.

## Example sentences:

- Quick! He's home!
- Where have you been?
- Your little brother did what?
- There's a hole in this boat.
- I think I'm going to faint.
- Did you bring the money?
- Will you marry me?
- Why don't you listen?
- Help!
- Ouch!
- What's that sound?
- Who was arrested?

## *Group Improvisation*

**Aim:** Students have to think on their feet while creating a "live" scene with other people.

**Time:** 10–15 minutes

**Preparation:** Make a handout containing the rules of the improvisation.

**Procedure:** First, tell the students that they are going to improvise a scene together. Ask them to think of a setting—for example, a bus stop or a cafeteria. The scene starts at that place, but can move to a different place if the participants wish. Next, discuss the rules:

1. Only four people can be in the scene at one time.
2. Actors have to make a clear entrance to and exit from the scene that makes sense.
3. Actors in the scene and those watching have to pay careful attention to what is happening.
4. Actors should not stay in the scene too long, but let everyone have a go.

5. Actors can go in and out of the scene as many times as they wish.

Four students volunteer to start the scene. This exercise works best if students go in and out of the scene frequently. If the scene starts to become stilted or boring, you can intervene by choosing four people to start a new scene in a different place.

The exercises in this chapter can be used at any stage of the drama class—at the very beginning of the course to set the atmosphere, and as warm-up exercises at the start of each rehearsal session. In addition, these exercises can be used in any language class.

# Chapter Three

## Texts: Finding and Modifying a Published Script or Writing an Original Script

We are often asked for help in finding a script, and it is true that we have old favorites that we pull off the shelves. However, every class is different. One class will like texts that other classes have done; another class will reject the old favorites, so we are constantly on the lookout for new material to create a large pool of plays from which to choose. We offer here some criteria for finding performable texts. We are sure that these will especially help teachers who are new to using drama/role-play in the classroom.

### What Kind of Script Should You Use?

Published plays by successful playwrights are often good sources of colloquial speech and models of natural language. (Skits that are written by English teachers to teach a grammar point, on the other hand, sometimes fall short of authentic language: real people having a real conversation.) As R. A. Via notes, "A successful playwright . . . is not concerned with the rules and regulations of English, pattern practice or in illustrating a particular structure, but in expressing ideas and feelings" (1976). One of our jobs as language teachers is to present good models to our students so that they can see and hear how to express their ideas and feelings. A good play would give you and your students lots of authentic language to work with. For classroom purposes, making minor changes to the play is not unusual—directors sometimes need to make adjustments.

## Criteria to Consider When Choosing a Play

### Appeal

The play should appeal to your students. Give your students several plays or scenes from plays to choose from. You want them to be enthusiastic about working on this project and if they are empowered to choose one or more for themselves, they will be more likely to throw themselves wholeheartedly into rehearsals. Additionally, if a play appeals to your students, it will probably be well received by their peers and thereby generate enthusiasm for the next time you teach that class.

### Fit

The play should fit your purposes. Sometimes we have chosen a play because we wanted the students to learn something in addition to experiencing the language. We sometimes incorporate a play into a theme the students are studying, such as social customs, or the justice system of the United States. Or we use a play as an opening into a difficult topic, for instance, how to talk about sexual expectations or parent–adult child problems or jealousy or grief.

### Length

The length of the play should fit into your time frame. In our Intensive English Program, we sometimes offer a whole class on drama. This allows the teacher and students to spend a seven-week session (one hour a day, five days a week) preparing a nearly full-scale production (see Chapter 1 for a discussion of this type of class). However, if a course is not totally devoted to drama, there may not be enough class time to cast and rehearse a full-length play for public performance. In these circumstances, it is best to choose a short play (a one-act), or to select a couple of scenes from a longer play and spend whatever time you feel you can (from several days to a couple of weeks). *Remember:* You don't have to perform a whole play.

### Parts

The play should not have one dominant part; as much as possible, the parts should be more or less equal in length. This is very important because if one character of a play or scene dominates the speaking, the rest of your actors can become bored or jealous. A discipline problem may result when too many of your actors are standing around offstage and unoccupied.

## Number of characters

The number and gender of the characters should nearly match those of your class

**Small number of parts—large class** You can sometimes work around having fewer characters in the play than you have students in your class by double-casting (two separate casts prepare the same scene). Or two separate casts could do two different scenes from the same play.

**Large number of parts—small class** When there are more characters than students, some students can double up and play two parts. In that case, the teacher's role is to help the students differentiate between the two characters that one student is acting. You also must check to see that the two characters do not appear on stage at the same time.

**More male characters than male class members or vice versa** You can cast females in male roles or the other way around, if the students are willing and the parts are not too dependent on gender specifics. For instance, we have produced the television play, *Twelve Angry Men*—originally written for an all-male cast—and had some women taking parts. To avoid confusion at production time, we changed the name to *Twelve Angry Jurors*. This television drama by Reginald Rose is an excellent choice for a class to work on. It is a three-act play, but written to fit into an hour program. Either men or women can play the characters, who are not given names, and you need make only a few minor changes to the language.

## The play's language

The play's language can be more difficult than the level of your class. You should not be afraid of challenging language. We do not mean that you should choose plays with archaic language. Most plays from the 1940s on to the present day will use contemporary language familiar to people in their teens to their sixties. If there are phrases here and there that could be considered quaint, the play probably will be better received if you eliminate or rewrite them. But don't be worried about your students memorizing language that they don't understand. They will enjoy the challenge and will eventually sort it out.

Beware of Shakespeare! You may want to use his plots and characters, but even native speakers need a lot of help and support when they first encounter his language.

## What about offensive language?

As to offensive language, many modern plays have language that your students will probably eventually see or hear, but you may not want to be the person who introduced them to it. We recommend that you consider rewriting the offensive phrases, or that you not use any play that has language that makes you uncomfortable.

## Royalties

A royalty is the fee paid to the owner of a copyright so that a theater can produce a play. If teachers use the play as one source in their second language classrooms, and/or if they offer the performance free of charge to other students and faculty for academic purposes, this is considered fair practice and there is no need to worry about fees. If, however, the school wishes to produce the play for a larger public and charge money, the director must write for permission to perform the chosen play and pay a royalty fee. If you have questions about royalty fees, you may find the answers to your questions in the information pages or websites of Samuel French, Dramatists Play Service, or Baker's Plays. Most of these services have e-mail addresses (for websites see bibliography).

## *Where Can You Find Plays?*

Libraries are the best place to start. You can search for a particular play by author, or by title. If you don't have a particular play in mind, and you just want to find something on a particular theme, say a holiday play, we suggest that you look in one of the play indexes or catalogs (see bibliography) under the name of the holiday. If all you want are a few short scenes, not about any particular theme, then we suggest that you look in books of scenes used for acting classes (see "Actors' Exercises, Improvisation, and Scripts" in the Bibliography). Once you find a book that has what you want, look around in that section of the library stacks. There may be other books nearby that would also serve your purpose. As you know, cataloguing systems (Library of Congress; Dewey Decimal) put related subjects together under the same number. If your library has a computerized catalog, you could do a keyword search similar to the one we show next. In this next section, we discuss putting together a good keyword search, finding scenes in audition books, using play indexes and catalogs to find an appropriate play, or discovering plays in collections.

## Keyword search

Searching a computerized catalog, you can find books containing a number of short dialogues by using such keyword terms as

> Acting exercises
>
> Audition scenes
>
> Monologues
>
> Skits
>
> Scenes for actors
>
> Rehearsal scenes
>
> Improvisation
>
> Improvised scenes
>
> Comedy sketches
>
> Role-play

Coming up with the best terms is crucial to the success of a search. Any keyword search that brings up hundreds of possibilities has not been narrowed down enough. "Drama in education" will, for instance, bring up books for elementary school as well as high school teachers (in our university library, this brought up 582 titles). At the end of this chapter we will list terms that we have used in our searches, but remember that each library may have chosen its own terms to designate various categories. We have found that the best policy is to 1. Look in the *Library of Congress Subject Headings* (five volumes) for possible categories, and 2. Ask a reference librarian for help in coming up with the most elegant terms (those terms that are neither too broad nor too narrow) and the best combination of terms.

## Scene books for actors' auditions

Your library may contain audition books that are designed for actors who are native speakers. These books are frequently used in drama/acting classes at high school, university, and professional levels. They can be useful for language classroom exercises as well. Audition books are filled with short scenes (probably no scene is longer than ten minutes). Each scene is usually self-contained (with a clear beginning, middle, and end) and lends itself well to classroom use and performances. Included are monologues, as well as dialogues for two or three or, sometimes, more actors.

Short scenes are much more manageable for first-time actors (and first-time drama teachers) than three- or four-act plays. We list a number of these audition books in the Bibliography. You should be able to locate some of them in your local library or, if you have access to one, a university library. In addition, your local bookstore may have some of the more recent ones on their shelves, or be willing to order one for you.

## Indexes

Play indexes are large reference books (noncirculating) in libraries. The indexes list plays by authors, by titles, by numbers of actors needed, and, generally, by subject matter (for instance, if you want a play about AIDS or a particular holiday). The descriptions of the plays are brief, usually only five to ten lines long.

The leading indexes follow:

- *Baker's Plays* is a catalogue that lists plays every year from Broadway, Off Broadway, the West-End (London), and the regional theaters of the United States. Plays are listed in the following categories: Professional, Full-length, One-act, Youth Theatre, Christmas, and Women's Theatre.

- *Dramatists Play Service* publishes a complete catalog in even years and a supplement in odd years. In the front of the index are listed the Pulitzer Prize play winners and the Tony Award plays. In addition to listing plays by title and by author, it lists plays by New Acquisitions, Full-length Plays, Short Plays, Musicals, and by Number of Characters.
- *Play Index* published every three or four years, lists by type (musicals, one-acts, television plays, puppet plays) and by gender and number (example: 1W plays = plays with a cast of one woman; 2M plays = plays with a cast of two men).
- Samuel French, Inc., publishes a *Catalogue of Plays and Musicals*. It lists plays by the following categories: Full-length Royalty, Low Royalty, Non Royalty, and Budget Plays; One-Act Royalty, Low Royalty, Non Royalty Plays; Musicals and Operettas; Theatre for Youth, Religious Plays, Monologues, Readings, Scenes, and Dialect Plays; and Anthologies. Cross-referencing is done for Theater Festivals; Mystery plays; Black, Chinese, Irish, and Jewish plays. Samuel French, Inc., is the largest publisher of individual paperback scripts (acting versions) for actors to use.

## Individual plays and play collections

**Search by playwright's name** Libraries and bookstores are sure to have some of the more famous playwrights' works represented. If you know their names, and the playwrights are well known (such as American playwrights Tennessee Williams, William Inge, Arthur Miller, Kaufman and Hart, or David Mamet), their work will undoubtedly be represented under their names. Some younger or less-well-known playwrights may not have individual plays published; however, editors may publish together in one volume several plays by a relatively unknown playwright. (This is discussed later in: "Search in collections.")

Once you know the Dewey classification number or the Library of Congress classification number for a particular playwright, you can go to that section of the library stacks and find other plays by that writer.

**Search by play's title** If you know a play by name, but don't know who the playwright is, you can check your local library or bookstores under the title of the play. However, many plays in bookstores or libraries are in anthologies and may not be published individually. Some anthologies are published by type of plays (Christmas plays) or by the year in which the play was performed, or by the country or region in which the play appeared.

**Search in collections.** Sometimes plays are not published singly nor are they included in a book of plays by one particular playwright. Other types of collections that you might look at:

1. If you know the year that the play was first performed, you might find it in *The Best Plays of (year)*.

2. If the play was performed at a regional theater, it might be published under that theater's name, or, if it was first performed at a festival, such as the Humana Festival of New Plays, in Louisville, Kentucky, it might appear in a collection under the title of the festival.

3. For plays about a region of the country, you might look under terms like *southern plays or playwrights* or *New England plays*.

## Other places to search

- When you just want some information about good plays and you do not have a specific play title that you want to find, check with local schools or universities to find out what plays they have performed recently. The information they give you may lead you to discover a contemporary playwright that you have not encountered before. The director may have an acting version of a recently produced play that you can borrow to find out if that play would be useful for your purposes.

### Theater Department/English Department Collections

- You might also check to see if there is a play library in the theater department of a nearby college. Some theater departments will donate a couple of scripts of a play that has recently been performed by the college to a departmental library. Additionally, you can talk with someone who has been a director of plays for the local community: they might be able to help you find a script that would fit your needs.

- Another source can be local teachers of English. They may have collected personal libraries of their own, or they might be able to supply you with names of plays and playwrights that have been of interest to their students.
- Check to see if your library subscribes to a monthly magazine called *American Theatre*. The complete text of a contemporary play often appears in this magazine.
- Use the Internet to get television scripts. There have been Internet websites that provided us with scripts. We have utilized a search engine with *scripts+(title of a TV show)* or *moviescripts* and discovered many scripts from television shows and old movies. Some of the sites had early scripts (not the final script of the particular show); some had transcriptions (the transcriber taped the show and later wrote out the script). *A word of caution:* In the wake of recent music/copyright investigations, we noticed that some of the sites we had used were closed. The legal issue regarding these sites is rather fluid at present and what is allowed now may change.

## Modifying Play Scripts

Even when you find a play that you like, the script may not exactly match your needs. Maybe there are too many or too few characters for your class size; maybe the play is too long. What can you do? In this section, we suggest how to modify a published play script to fit your needs.

Sometimes you find a script that is almost right for your class. You think with a little revising, it would be perfect. We usually revise a script when it calls for more characters than we have in a particular class or when the whole play would be too much for our students to memorize.

If the script is too long, you can investigate modifying it with your class (or on your own, if you don't have time to work with your class) in the following ways:

- Modifying by eliminating one character or combining two characters into one

- Eliminating a scene
- Replacing a scene with a summary of action to be delivered by a narrator
- Paraphrasing a scene (changing the dialogue into simplified language)

## Method One: Modifying Number of Characters or Scenes

### Students read text

Students read the chosen text—preferably, no more than one act (first, aloud and afterward, to themselves). Have the whole class make a list of the sequence of events.

### Divide into groups

Divide your class into several groups, having each group decide if they will add or take away characters, to match the number of students in the class/group.

- If there are more characters in the text than students in your class, combine two characters into one—or eliminate a minor character.
- If there is the right number of characters, but more males than females and your class is mostly females, sometimes an Uncle Ed can become an Aunt Edwina without too much trouble.
- When the scene is too short and there aren't enough characters to fit the number of students in your class, have students write in as many characters as needed. For instance, students could imagine a second prince in the *Cinderella* story: he would wildly change the story as the two brothers fight over Cinderella and she stands tapping her foot in the corner.

### Students choose parts

Within groups, students can choose parts that interest them. Each group should choose a section of the play that interests the members of that group. Groups then improvise dialogues for those sections, with each person being responsible for remembering the specific part that he or she improvised.

## Rewrite

Finally, each group should rewrite its section(s) with words and phrases that the students feel comfortable using.

### *Method Two: Modifying by Eliminating Lines or Scenes*

Divide the class into groups and ask that they decide if there are any scenes that could be left out of the presentation. If students cannot eliminate a whole scene, help them to summarize lines within a scene so that they could be delivered by a narrator. It may also be possible for a narrator to summarize a whole section of the play. (A summary is usually shorter than a performed scene.) One class modified a story in the following manner: in some versions of the Cinderella story, a messenger arrives and announces a Royal Ball. The following scene has a dancing master and a seamstress. There were not enough students to take on these parts, so the class decided to have the scenes with the dancing master and the seamstress narrated by the Storyteller who opened and ended the play. That scene was shortened to one sentence: "A seamstress was hired to make the sisters new dresses and a dancing master came to give them dancing lessons."

### *Method Three: Modifying by Paraphrasing a Scene*

Have students read a scene and talk about the general meaning.

Once we had students struggle with a selection from the play *Whose Life Is It Anyway?* by Brian Clark. The language was a challenge and after the first reading, the students groaned that they did not understand anything. However, by answering a few general questions, such as "Where does the scene take place?" "Who is Ken?" and "Who is Mrs. B.?" they discovered that they understood more than they had thought. They understood that it was taking place, probably, in a hospital; that Ken had suffered some sort of physical trauma and that Mrs. B. was a nurse or some sort of hospital employee.

Students, in pairs, read aloud the dialogue, looked at the meaning, *line by line*, and, if they disagreed on the meaning, they negotiated between them what they thought each line meant. This was the toughest part of this assignment and took a full class period (for some pairs, longer). We asked them to look beyond the words, to try to get at the feelings that were under the surface. Not what did Mrs. B. say, but what did Mrs. B. want to accomplish? What did Ken want?

Once students feel that they understand the meanings, encourage them to improvise the dialogue in their own words. When students are satisfied that their improvisation contains all the information that is contained in the original, they can choose a person to be the group scribe, who will then begin to record the paraphrased dialogue on paper.

The last part of our exercise with *Whose Life Is It Anyway?* consisted in pairs rewriting the dialogue in their own words. The dialogues were very different from each other, but each pair's improvisations were very meaningful to the students who had struggled to come up with a good expression of the ideas. This class never gave a formal performance for other classes of the scenes they had rewritten, but they performed with passion for each other.

## Writing Your Own Texts

### *The Major Ingredients for Writing a Play*

This is a good place to talk about writing your own text. First, you do not need to start out to write a full three-act play with your students. Start small, with short dialogues and, if the students get really interested in one, follow it through; it may grow into four or five scenes.

As we said earlier in this chapter, dialogues in texts written for language classes are not necessarily dramatic. They are basically constructions of conversations to illustrate a grammar point or to introduce new vocabulary and structures. For a dialogue to be dramatically interesting, there must be some sort of *characterization* and some point of *conflict*. For example, when students are writing a play and they put two people in a room together and give them a simple dialogue (typically what appears in language texts)—it is boring. Put two people in a room together and one of them wants to talk and the other does not—the conflict makes it more interesting. Give each person a personality and the reasons why one wants to talk and the other one does not—a deeper, more interesting dialogue will emerge.

For example: there are two men in prison. Character A wants to know where Character B hid the money and jewelry they stole together; Character B doesn't want to tell him. Character B wants to keep the money; Character A wants to give the stolen money to someone he loves (who was wronged by Character B). The tension between the conflicting desires of the characters is what makes the writing fun and demands that the students who write the script, as well as the eventual audience, pay attention.

The trick to getting your students to write interesting dialogues is first to get them to be interested in the characters and the situation. We usually start out with the whole class contributing ideas and someone at the board recording the suggestions. The teacher may interject a question or encouragement from time to time, as in the following example.

*Teacher:* What would you like to write a dialogue about?

*Student 1:* The food at the dorms. (Student 2, at board, writes, *food, dorm*).

*Teacher:* What about the food?

*Students:* It is terrible. (Student at board writes *terrible*).

*Teacher:* If everyone feels the same, where is the conflict? Who causes the conflict in our little drama? (Student 2 writes *who* and *conflict*).

*Student 1:* Most of us.

*Student 2:* No, Thomas: he thinks the food is great!

*Student 3:* No, I nominate Roberta: she never eats anything.

*Teacher:* We need to decide who the play is about, what the story line could be, and how we go about telling it.

## *Starting from Scratch: Ingredients for a Good Play*

We discuss a possible story and write on the board (see Figure 3–1.)

At an early point, we stop the whole class discussion. With the students in groups, we tell each group to work out a plot (the shape of the story line or what happens) using the ingredients that we have written on the board.

## Plot

Playwrights start with a "seed" *situation* that leads into the plot, or the skeleton of the story. Each group should think of itself as a playwright and decide for itself what happens to whom from the first moment to the last. The "seed" from the preceding classroom discussion could be that a girl doesn't eat. You might think that a story about the dorm food would not be interesting, but when we ask our students "Why?" many times, a creative plot does usually emerge.

## Characters

The writers need to consider the number and type of *characters* (the number of students in the group is a possible number, unless one of them does not want to act and prefers to direct) that will be in their play. In the dorm scenario, who else besides Thomas and Roberta interact with them? Confidants? Professors? Doctors? Parents? Siblings?

After the students decide on the types of characters that will be in their dialogue, they must flesh out the personalities and relationships between the characters.

## Relationships

To help your students make their characters interesting, ask questions. How well do the characters know each other? Have they just met? What do they know about Roberta, the girl who doesn't eat? Who knows what her problem is? Who wants to help and why? If the characters know each other well, how is this made clear to an audience through language? Is the language abbreviated? Are there terms of endearment used?

Figure 3–1: Essentials of a Play

| Characters | Plot | Action |
|---|---|---|
| Number and relationships | Beginning situation<br><br><br><br><br><br>Middle conflicts | |
| | | |
| | Conclusion | |
| | | |

Characters—who they are and what the relationships are of one to the others.

Dialogue—what the characters say to each other

Plot—what happens overall

Motivations—reasons for what is said or what happens

Conflict—tension that holds the play together

Actions and consequences of actions

## Conflict

What does each character want? Are their desires in conflict with each other? If a boy and girl are sweethearts, where is the conflict? Has it been influenced by someone to whom they owe obedience? Does it have to do with age differences? Or religion? Or difference in social expectations? Not all conflicts are easy to visualize. Words are the main carriers of meaning, but the playwright can also specify actions. There are subtle movements of head, hands, shoulders that signal a character's acceptance or rejection of another's ideas. For instance, Character A suggests going to see a psychiatrist and Character B is hurt by such a suggestion. Ask your students how they would respond nonverbally. Some may sigh and roll their eyes skyward. Others may clench and unclench their hands or shake their heads. Students can include these directions in the script.

## Actions

The student writers must decide movement on and off the stage: why a character enters or exits—and when, and where each character is in relation to every other character during each scene. You can demonstrate how sitting or standing shows relationships. After students decide on the sequence of actions, they need to divide their play into scenes.

## Motives

Let us consider the preceding set of student-generated facts about the dorm food. There wasn't much to go on. There was an interesting "seed," but what was the conflict that could develop into an interesting story? Perhaps a character's motives would give the plot some direction.

What was the reason for the one girl's not eating? Was she trying to get the attention of a certain young male she knows? Or maybe she wanted the sympathy of her professor? Perhaps she was overweight and the victim of teasing. Or maybe she wanted to go home. And who reveals this to the audience? Do two of her friends discuss their worry for her health when she isn't there to defend herself? And does she come in while they are talking about her? We teachers act as the goad—asking the writers questions while they think out the plot, the characters, and their relationships, action by action, examining motives and changes in feelings. (*A word of wisdom: It is better to abandon a topic that isn't going anywhere than to struggle on until students lose interest.*)

## Playwriting Conventions (the Format of Dialogue)

Another area that students might need help with is the format of a written dialogue. Two conventions are generally followed.

## Example 1

A character's name is usually written on the left of the page just before his or her lines. Directions to the actors are enclosed in parentheses and/or written in italics.

*Mr. Barkis:* Is this your first time in London, David?

*David:*     Yes, sir. It's my first journey anywhere. (*He nervously twists his sleeve.*)

## Example 2

Sometimes the character's name is in the middle of the page, with the character's speaking line below it. The directions to the actors may be in italics and also centered.

Mr. Barkis
Is this your first time in London, David?
David
Yes, sir. It's my first journey anywhere.
*He nervously twists his sleeve.*

Your students may want to include stage directions (these suggestions of actions, such as *he nervously twists his sleeve,* or *coughs,* are not spoken). Sometimes these are written in parentheses, and sometimes they are written in italics, or both.

## How to Get Started: Generating Ideas for Dialogues

You and your students will need a starting point from which to generate ideas. The stimulus may come from something like the

70

preceding class interaction; from *written stimuli,* such as other forms of literary work (novels, short stories, folktales, letters, poetry, song lyrics, newspaper/magazine articles, unfinished stories); from *visual stimuli,* such as paintings, movies, or television; from *audio stimuli,* such as the sound of a train in the distance, an emergency vehicle siren, or birds singing; or from *research projects* you may assign your class to investigate. No matter what the stimulus, we generally begin with a whole-class discussion, then break the class up into groups to let the students improvise dialogues related to the stimulus. Lastly, we ask that each group put the dialogue into some sort of permanent form by writing it or recording it on tape. We may vary this approach or add to it from time to time.

## Written stimuli

You may want to convert novels, short stories, and folktales into plays (taking the characters and the story line and writing a series of dialogues to tell it).

### Method

1. Teachers print out very abbreviated versions of several stories. After the students have read all the stories, have the class vote on which one they like best.

2. Using the chosen story, the whole group or class contributes to working out the storyboard. (See Figure 3–2.) A storyboard is the skeleton of the story that is divided into scenes and written in two halves. The left half is the designation of the cast and action of each scene. The right half is the dialogue. Take, for example, *Cinderella.* Most Westerners are familiar with the story: Cinderella is a young girl whose stepmother and two stepsisters treat her terribly. The prince invites all the young women of the town to a ball, but the stepmother ignores Cinderella's pleas to go. Her fairy godmother comes to her rescue, magically giving her a magnificent dress, carriage and horses, and footmen, but also warning her that she must leave the ball before midnight. Cinderella dances with the prince at the ball. She forgets to leave on time and, in running away so that the prince will

not see her turn back into a ragged, dirty girl, she loses her slipper. The prince uses the slipper to identify her and takes her away to marry her.

The group must then answer a number of questions:

How many characters are necessary to act out this story?

Minimum: Cinderella, stepsisters, fairy godmother, prince

Maximum: In addition, father, stepmother, servants, and so on

How many scenes are necessary to tell this story?

- Scene 1: daytime, invitation arrives; we meet Cinderella and her two stepsisters in their home
- Scene 2: at Cinderella's home, night of the ball; getting dressed; Cinderella's disappointment and the arrival of the fairy godmother
- Scene 3: at the ball, just before midnight, Cinderella is a sensation and is dancing with the prince when she remembers she must leave
- Scene 4: the search of the prince for Cinderella, in Cinderella's home

The whole class has to decide what to tell the audience and by what means—through narrative or dialogue or actions or some combination of the three before the writing of the storyboard (see Figure 3–2) can begin. For example,

The teacher asks: "How does the audience know about the invitation? Is it on a piece of paper? The audience cannot read it, so how do they find out what it says? Does a narrator tell? Does a servant of the prince deliver it and proclaim it? Do the sisters talk of it?"

The students decide that a messenger from the king and queen comes to the house and announces that there will be a ball. They decide that people couldn't read and had to have such announcements proclaimed.

Figure 3–2: Storyboard for *Cinderella*

On the blackboard, the teacher can draw a vertical line from the top to the bottom.

| On the left of this line he or she can write: | On the right of this line he or she can write: |
|---|---|
| | |

Scene 1

| Characters: Cinderella, two stepsisters | Dialogue |
|---|---|
| Action:<br>Sisters enter. | SS1: Oh ho! We have an invitation to the ball! Little Miss Smudgeface has to stay home and take care of the house. |
| Sisters show off new dresses. | SS2: You don't get a new dress and we do. |
| Sisters tease Cinderella, pulling at her rags. | Cindy: When my father hears how cruel you are to me, he will help me, I'm sure.<br><br>SS1 & SS2: Don't be too sure Little Grubbyhands; it would take a week to clean you up! |
| Sisters laugh and leave the room. Cindy cries. Suddenly a fairy godmother enters. | FG: Don't cry! Wipe your tears away and go get a pumpkin. We have work to do to get ready |

And so continue on, creating the characters and actions for each scene on the left side of the vertical line. The dialogue can be fleshed out at a later time on the right side of the board.

Here are a few other stories that we have liked that could be used in this exercise:

"The Unicorn in the Garden" by James Thurber

"The Tell-Tale Heart" by Edgar Allen Poe

"The First Day of School" by William Saroyan

"The Monkey's Paw" by W. W. Jacobs

## Using a letter to create a dialogue

### Method

1. Present a letter that has many missing letters. (It can be printed on paper or written on the blackboard by the teacher.) See the letter from an American soldier during World War II in "Geographica: People, Places, and Creatures of Our Universe" in the *National Geographic,* November 2001.

2. The students are given a letter that has been partially destroyed. For example (see Figure 3–3):

Figure 3–3: Letter with Missing Words and Letters

| |
|---|
| Dear S _____, |
| I am so s _____ that _____ |
| When we last _____ I couldn't _____. |
| Do you think _____ ? I wish _____. |
| Please, send me _____. If you cannot _____, |
| let me _____. |
| With great _____, |

3. Individually, students study the surviving fragments, creating their own contexts.

4. Individually, students can think about the following:

   • How does the letter get damaged? Is it torn? burned? water damaged?

   • Who wrote the letter? And who is the intended receiver? What is their relationship?

   • What happens in a scene before the writing of the letter? Does it explain why it was written?

   • What could happen in a scene where the letter is found? Is the finder innocent of the context?

   • What could happen in a scene where the letter writer finds out that the letter survives? Who tells of its existence?

5. Divide the class into groups. The students within a group can share their completed letters and scenarios with other members of the group. Then the group can choose one student's ideas and improvise a dialogue. For instance, one group may choose to do the scene before the writing of the letter; another may choose the scene that takes place after the damaged letter is found. The two scenes do not have to be related. Before the groups can improvise the dialogue, they need to make some decisions. Each group must decide *who* is in their play, what is the *relationship* of one to another, and what *conflict* drives the *actions* that take place during their scene.

   Group 1: The scene that takes place before the writing of a letter: They decide who is in the scene—for example, a father, a daughter and a son. They decide what the letter said before it was partially destroyed and fit appropriate words into the gaps in the writing. They then choose the background for the letter: that the daughter has made a request, the father refused the request of the daughter, and the son supports the daughter, his sister. They decide what the request was, which one of the three had the best motive for writing the letter, and for whom the letter was meant.

*We like to remind students that in a dialogue, the actors must say enough to make the conflict understandable, but they don't have to tell everything.*

Group 2: Discussing the scene after the letter is discovered. Students talk about the background of the letter. Why was it written and by whom? Students decide what the letter says (filling in the gaps) and then who is in the scene: the letter writer? the intended receiver of the letter?

The teacher asks: "Does the relationship between your characters change after the discovery of the letter? How?"

6. After making their choices, the groups then begin to improvise a dialogue. Improvising should at first be done without any writing. This allows the group to explore with more freedom than if they were writing down every word. Students are not happy erasing great chunks of their work, so we find they are more satisfied if they don't write until they have improvised a scene more than once.

7. Writing the scene. The students can choose one person in their group to be the scribe. We usually suggest that the designated scribe be someone with legible handwriting and that a second person in the group type it up and either email it or copy it and give it to the other members. Problems can arise with having only one person responsible for the typing and distributing: that person may not show up for the class the next time (or whenever the script is due) and then that group does not have a script. On the other hand, if everyone is responsible for writing down his or her own words, no one person has the whole script. We have had groups where everyone in the group wrote down all the lines, but nominated one person to do the typing. This method may seem cumbersome, and there are always a few students who don't get all the words, but the whole group can still function if one member is missing.

## Creating a new play by changing the ending of a story
The teacher prints out a story. The story can be a well-

known fairy tale, such as *Goldilocks and the Three Bears*, the plot of *Romeo and Juliet*, a movie synopsis, or a personal story.

## Method

1. Students read the printout a couple of times (individual, silent reading).

2. In groups, students discuss possible alternative endings. (See "Essentials of a Play" Figure 3–1.) They need to recognize how the conflict logically might be resolved and then talk about how it could be resolved differently to make it funny or perhaps scary.

3. Each group improvises the final scene, beginning from the point at which the imagined new ending diverges from the story.

4. Each group writes a dialogue with the different ending.

## Creating a play from an unfinished story

## Method

1. The teacher hands out a brief story, but leaves off the ending.
2. Students in groups decide what the ending will be.
3. Students then write dialogue for the whole scene.

> Example: Duck Takes a Swim
> A family is waiting at the airport hotel for the limousine to take them to the airport. The father is paying the bill for the night's stay. The mother and three children are near the door with the suitcases. All are dressed in their best clothes. The two older children are treating the shiny marble floor as a slide. The youngest child, a little girl who is three, is standing by the lobby pool, her stuffed toy duck hanging from her right hand. Suddenly she raises her right arm and says, "Duck, swim."

The teacher asks, "What do you think happens next?"

**Students create a dialogue from a newspaper account of an incident** The teacher suggests ways of using the information in an article that the students read. For example: Write a possible interview with someone in the story (a victim/the discoverer/ a witness).

> *Example:* (from the June 22, 2000, *The Herald-Times*, (Bloomington, Indiana). The newspaper reports that a woman was charged with attacking a teenager with a frozen turkey. The teenager told the police that he was outside this woman's home, working on a muffler with a friend. The woman came out of her home yelling at the boy. He said that she dropped a frozen turkey on his head. The boy then picked up the turkey and threw it through the front window. The woman told the police that the boy was wearing a pair of shoes that belonged to her, and that she offered to swap the turkey breast for the shoes. The newspaper said the "scuffle" erupted after the boy threw the turkey through the window. These are the actions. We do not know anything about the motivations and there was no follow-up article in later papers about this incident.

Method

1. Creating characters: the woman, the boy, the police investigator, others?

2. Developing motivation: what is the relation of the boy to the woman? Why is she yelling at him? Why is he wearing a pair of her shoes?

3. Setting: a police station, or a courtroom

4. Details: does the boy tell the same story as the woman? How does it end?

**Song lyrics or poetry** Holiday parties are good places for having a class perform before their peers. After studying a unit on poetry, your students could write their own poems about the change of seasons, or the friends they have made. One December we had a class present *'Twas the Night Before Christmas*. Each student had been given four lines of the long poem to memorize, two in the early part of the poem and two in the later part. Of course, in addition, each had to know the cue lines (the lines spoken just before that person was to speak)—a good listening exercise.

At the same holiday party, all students were given a printout of the words to the "Twelve Days of Christmas" and everyone joined in the singing. Certain people were given large signs depicting the words of the song—for instance, a large picture of a golden ring. When they heard the words *"five golden rings,"* five students held up the cards with a golden ring painted on it, and so on with all twelve days' signs.

There are many songs that tell stories and there are many ways that students can create a dialogue from one of these story songs. A good listening project for the students can be to listen repeatedly to the song and write down the words as they understand them. They then can write a dialogue to fit the story. The last "act" can be to hear the song played and, as the singer sings the songs, the students can mime action that fits the words of the song. Alternatively, one student can be the "singer" and say the words to the song and the other students can mime the actions.

## Visual stimuli

Creating a play from visual stimuli, such as movies, photographs or paintings, and television rather than creating something from the written word, allows your students' imaginations to be sparked by something that is visually striking or puzzling or appealing to the emotions. *Teachers: Always, always review the visual so that you know it well.*

**Movies** Choose a movie scene. You can focus on a particular conflict that is thought provoking; a whole movie might be overwhelming.

> Example 1: A movie scene can start the students thinking about a particular theme. The film *Dead Man Walking* can open up the topic of the death penalty. There are a couple scenes where the nun, hoping to help him face his punishment, talks with the prisoner. Students can discuss the pros

79

and cons of the death sentence, after which they might find it interesting to write a dialogue showing the prisoner in a different light, or a dialogue between the prisoner and a journalist after he has talked with the nun.

Example 2: Sometimes it is fun to mock a movie that is very popular. When everyone was talking about *Titanic*, one class decided to do a parody of this very popular movie. The students picked several scenes and rewrote them, poking fun at the very dramatic moments. The audience reaction was wild with laughter when a female student who was normally very quiet began to hack the air with a paper axe in order to save the young man who was handcuffed to a pipe.

Example 3: You can show a scene from a silent movie or a movie with the sound turned off and you could ask that your class come up with a dialogue that fits the action.

**Pictures** Choose a painting or a photograph that tells a story. (*Sources:* Our university School of Education Library has prints of famous paintings and photographs that are available for teachers to borrow for classroom use. Also our community library lends paintings to the public. And, of course, magazines sometimes have illustrations and pictures. *If you wish to make copies, be sure to check the quality of the picture. Some pictures do not have enough contrast to copy well.*)

Example 1: Photographers or painters try to capture a single moment. Students can fashion a dialogue around that moment: the lone boy standing in front of a tank in Tienamen Square or the Victory Day sailor's kiss. Teachers can ask, "What do you see? What do you think led up to this moment? What do you think will happen afterward?" The students can improvise a beginning or an end.

Example 2: Many of Norman Rockwell's paintings were designed to tell a story. For example, one of his most famous paintings is based on a true incident from the civil rights era. In 1964, he painted *The Problem We All Live With* for *Look* magazine, showing eight-year-old Ruby Bridges walking to school in New Orleans between United States marshals. This can be a good starting point for a dialogue; students can share reactions to the painting. *Girl with Black Eye* by Norman Rockwell shows a girl who is waiting to talk with the principal of her school; her facial expression and those expressions on the faces beyond the open door might inspire a lively dialogue.

**Television** Teacher tapes a scene from a situation comedy for the class to view together.

## Method

1. *First day:*
   - The whole class views the scene and discusses the plot (what happened to whom)
   - In small groups, the students reenact the scene
2. *Second day:*
   - In small groups have the students improvise a scene they think may have come before the scene they viewed.
   - In small groups, the students act out what they think may follow the scene they have viewed.
   - Students share their ideas for improvisation with the other groups.
3. *Third day:*
   - If students are interested, have them write the prescene or postscene that they have improvised, to be handed in.
   - Students perform prescenes, reenact the scene that they viewed, and perform postscenes. This gives them an overview of the flow of the little drama that they have concocted.
   - We always consider the possibility of a public performance (for another class, or for the whole Intensive English Program). Much depends on the enthusiasm of the students for the work that they have created.

## Creating a dialogue from research projects

**Information gathered by the students** There is sometimes information that we want the students to know and, rather than handing out a paper with the information already written up for them, we ask that students go out into the community and get the information for themselves. Such information includes:

- How to get a driver's license
- How to open a bank account
- How an international student can work: what are the steps in the process?
- What to do if a student gets a parking ticket or gets arrested
- What health facilities are available and how to pay for services
- How to deal with harassment by fellow students or by strangers
- What students should do if they lose their passport
- What to do if a police car is following them with flashing lights, or if there is an emergency vehicle with flashing lights and sounding horn heading toward them

Here are some suggestions on how students can write a dialogue based on the information that they have gathered.

## Method

*First day:*

1. Ask students for their preferences: what would they like to investigate? We have had individual students ask about the laws governing getting married in our state, how Americans get divorced, or how to file a claim in a court.

2. Discuss with students where they must go to get the information or give them telephone numbers and direct them to get the information by telephone.

3. Help the students to come up with a good sentence or two to introduce themselves, so that the business or office will understand that this is a class exercise and that the student is gathering information for the purpose that you devise.

4. Discuss with students how to ask good questions and have the students write out the questions that they will use.

82

5. Direct students to write out the answers that they receive, and/or to take along a tape recorder, so that they can be sure to get the correct information to present to the class.

*Second day or the day after the student interviews have been completed:*

6. Individual formal presentations of the information to the whole class.

7. After all the presentations are given, groups are formed and they share additional information within their groups (factual presentations). They are told that they must come up with a dialogue that will inform others in the program about what they have discovered. Students are doing no writing yet.

*Third day (They improvise dialogue—no writing yet.):*

8. The teacher goes from group to group and hears what the group has done so far. The teacher tells the students that everybody in the class already knows the information they are working with, so they need to be inventive (or else when they present their dialogue, the class will be bored). The teacher makes suggestions about how they could make their work more interesting. The teacher also suggests how they can incorporate this information into a telephone conversation with their mother or father back home.

Example 1: One class group was working on information about what to do if a student gets sick. They didn't know how to work the health center costs or hours into the dialogue. They decided that one student in the group had to be sick and that this girl's mother had just arrived from Korea. The mother gave the daughter a hug and said something like, "Oh, you must have a fever. We go to the hospital." Others in the group portrayed roommates and offered what they knew about the services that were available on the campus and how much cheaper it was to go to the health center than to call an ambulance to go to the emergency room of the local hospital. One of the students knew that patients need cash for whatever services you receive and that the patient would need to keep the receipt for reimbursement from the insurance company. For some students in the class this was a surprise; they had not been sick nor needed these services and might have made some costly choices if they had not been exposed to this little drama.

Example 2: One group was talking about getting a social security number in order to be able to work. They decided to make their dialogue a telephone conversation between a son who was in a university in the United States and his worried mother who was in Malaysia. But what made their play fun was that his little brother answered the phone first and could talk only about his expectation that the older brother was going to earn enough money to buy him a bicycle. When the mother was saying goodbye after a serious talk with her son, the younger brother grabbed the telephone to remind his brother about getting him a bicycle. They incorporated the research that they had done, but added a humorous touch and everyone in the class loved that little play.

## Audio stimuli

There are a number of ways to create a play from audio stimuli:

- From spoken stories by students or stories told on audio-tape
- From titles spoken by the teacher
- From random situations
- From anecdotes about cultural misunderstandings
- From music
- From sound effects

Stories told by students or teachers sometimes spark a reaction in the hearers and may produce a good dialogue. We think it works best if the teacher models by telling a story of his or her own first, so that the class gets the structure.

**Childhood stories** We have asked that students recall a favorite story from their childhoods. It is quite common for their stories to reflect the type of story that the teacher has told. For instance, when one of the teachers told of falling down a dam when she was ten years old, the stories that that experience brought out were generally stories of when the students as children did very daring and even dangerous things, but came through it all OK.

**Ghost stories** Sometimes around Hallowe'en, we tell an Edgar Allen Poe story ("The Tell-Tale Heart") or a shortened version of "The Legend of Sleepy Hollow" (by Washington Irving). These stories evoke tales of the supernatural from some of the students.

**Titles** We sometimes tell the students a title and ask them to come up with a dialogue that fits that title (for example: "Jealousy, the green-eyed monster," "My little brother's most embarrassing moment," or "My favorite holiday," or "The overheard telephone conversation").

**Situations** Sometimes, just describing a situation provides the seed for a productive role-play.
Method: Teacher recites situations for the students from which they are to construct a dialogue. The class is divided into groups, each group receiving a different situation.

Group 1:    Teacher says, "Person A is living in an apartment building. Every morning, Neighbor B picks up A's newspaper from in front of his door. A never has a newspaper to read. One day A finally has had enough of this." Students decide what A does and says and to whom. (Perhaps A complains to his own wife who advises him; perhaps he complains to Neighbor C; perhaps he complains directly to Neighbor B; perhaps he complains to Neighbor B's wife or child.) After they create the plot, they can act out the whole scene with improvised dialogue.

Group 2:    Person C has just had a telephone call from his mother that she is coming right over in a taxi to see him. He has five minutes to be ready to greet her.

Students must create the motives of the mother. They also are free to create the hour of the call, the willingness (or unwillingness) of the son to let her in, or any additional circumstances, such as other people involved. After the improvisation, the students write the dialogue.

Group 3:  You are at a party. You came with a very good friend, who has by now had too much to drink. How do you persuade him to let you drive him home? Everyone in the group has to contribute something. After the improvisation the students write the dialogue.

Group 4:  You have had an accident with your father's car. You come into your family home after everyone is asleep. What do you do? (We have used this last example just before a big vacation when students may be driving various places in the United States and may know some of the laws, but are not always aware of what is required of them if there is damage to another person's vehicle.)

1. Procedure for Group 4. Give the students a rough idea of what time it is (late) and that one of them has driven home in the father's damaged car. The other students in the group are family members. Tell the late student to wake up one family member and tell that person what has happened and ask what to do next.

2. No matter whom the student wakes up to tell, that person must give some advice to the first student. (Most of our students have opted to tell a little brother or sister first.)

3. At some point the teacher may interject that the student must wake up the father and tell him.

4. What is the father's first reaction? (We had one class where the father first asked about his car, which prompted the teacher to ask, "Aren't you worried about your son (your daughter)? Was he or she hurt?") If the father doesn't ask

the son (or daughter) if the police were called, that is the point where the teacher can caution students about the laws of the state in which they are living. In our state of Indiana, the law requires that in any accident where the damage is more than $500 the driver must call the police and stay with the car to make a report to the officer who responds to the call. The smallest scratch on a fender will probably cost more than $500 and many students are not aware of this. We tell our students that insurance companies will ask to see the police report before they agree to pay for damages.

We suggest that the group then act out all the action and dialogue. When the groups are satisfied that they have included the important facts, they may write their dialogue and practice it to perform it for other classes. Each group can become an ambassador of safety information to the other classes in our Intensive English Program.

**Cultural misunderstandings** Creating a play from incidents about cultural misunderstandings allows students to discuss things that trouble them. Working on scenes where the troubling incident can be explored by a group of people who trust each other can be very helpful in adjusting to a new culture.

### Method: Students share stories and then write about them

1. Students in small groups share a story of cultural friction where they were the ones who unknowingly committed a faux pas.

2. Students in small groups construct a scene where someone from the second language culture does something considered rude in the student's own culture.

3. Students in small groups share a funny or frightening incident in their lives that occurred because one or the other participant didn't understand the cultural signals of the place where they were living.

**Creating a dialogue after hearing music** The teacher explains to the students that they have just been hired to choose the music for a new film.

### Method

1. Have the students close their eyes and listen to a piece of music and then describe the situation and action that would fit the music. Have them listen to fast music, slow music, classical music, or popular music, with or without words. Do they see this as background music for a sad story? A funny story? A love story? A scary story? An adventure story? A cops and robbers story?

2. Have them write a scene to go with the piece of music they choose. This is an individual assignment, although it might work as a class project.

**Using sound effects to create a drama** In our local city/county library, there are sound effects sets. One is on long-play records, but the latest set (by the British Broadcasting Corporation) is on CDs—some forty or more—everything from nature sounds (waves on the seashore, thunder, rain) to animal sounds (dogs, cats, horses) to mechanical sounds (cars, airplanes, household appliances). You can borrow a CD of train whistles, foghorn, fire or police sirens, bird sounds, children laughing, a telephone ringing: these sounds sometimes evoke a memory or help a student construct a scene that will eventually grow into a play.

## A Few Final Words About Scripts

We feel strongly that encouraging students to act out a script (whether it was written by them or is a play by an established playwright, exposing them to new vocabulary and syntax) is a terrific language exercise—perhaps an exercise that students will put more of themselves into than any other. Therefore, finding or writing a script that excites your students' imaginations will draw them into an enriched language learning experience.

We hope that you will take some of these ideas and build on them. As you gain experience, your confidence in being able to guide your students through the brambles of writing a script will grow.

Here is a list of keywords to use in looking for scripts in an electronic catalog:

Acting exercises

Creative teaching methods

Dialogues

Drama

Drama and foreign language learning

Drama and teaching aids

Drama in language education

Improvisations

Language fluency using drama

Monologues

One act plays

Play scripts

Play writing

Role-play

Scenes for acting

Scripts and foreign language

Skits

# Chapter Four

## Page to Stage

Now that you have chosen a text for your drama class, it is time to decide what to do with it. In this chapter we will take you through the steps starting from an intensive read-through of the text (the page) to the performance itself (the stage).

For clarity and convenience, we have arranged the steps in the order we normally follow and numbered them in sequence. This is not an invariable formula; you can take what you wish from our suggested order. A rule of thumb is to watch your students and talk to them to find out what they like or dislike, what they find easy or difficult, and what they need to work on.

We divided the steps into four sections: "Decisions, decisions"; "Text work"; "Rehearsals"; and "Performance details." These sections have worked best for us if we followed them in the order written. Within those sections, however, we feel there is more flexibility. In "Decisions, decisions," we focus on some important decisions you need to make before launching into rehearsals. In "Text work," we concentrate on reading and analyzing the script, assigning roles, and memorizing lines. In "Rehearsals," we look at the nitty-gritty of acting: saying the lines, working with facial expressions and posture, looking at how and when to move. In "Performance details," we discuss using props, costumes, or scenery and look at the last-minute details before a performance. We also include time for debriefing the students after the performance: a critical look at the performance.

We have outlined these steps for your convenience:

## Decisions, decisions

Step 1    The big decision
Step 2    Smaller decisions

## Text work

Step 3    Basic theater terms and text format
Step 4    General read-through
Step 5    Text analysis
Step 6    Assigning roles
Step 7    In-depth read-through
Step 8    Memorizing lines

## Rehearsals

Step 9    Voice
Step 10   Timing and speed of delivery
Step 11   Facial expressions
Step 12   Gestures
Step 13   Posture
Step 14   Movement

## Performance details

Step 15   Preperformance details
Step 16   Postperformance

Some of the exercises in this chapter require a text. We will illustrate the text exercises with examples from *Nosey Busy Body* (see Appendix 2 for the complete script). You can, of course, adapt these exercises to suit any text your class is using.

When we use the word *play* in this chapter, unless otherwise specified, we are referring to the text that is being used in the class to prepare for a performance. By *on stage* we mean the space you will use for a performance.

# Decisions, decisions

## *Step 1: The Big Decision*

Once you and your students have chosen a text, you need to decide what to do with it. You have to make a big decision: Will you put on a small-scale performance or a large-scale performance? If you write your own text, you should probably decide this before actually writing the text (see Chapter 3 for suggestions on writing your own text).

## Small-scale performance versus large-scale performance

By *small-scale performance* we mean your class prepares two or more short texts: skits or scenes from a longer play for performance for other class members or for an invited audience at any time during the course. The students are divided into small groups and each group works with one skit or scene.

By *large-scale performance* we mean your whole class works with one longer text: a one-, two-, or three-act play. The students are not divided into small groups, but rather work as one large group with all of them taking one or more roles in the play that is to be performed at the end of the course.

### Pros of a small-scale performance

1. The whole production can be put together in a short period of time.

2. During rehearsals students work in small groups; each group works on its own play. Moving from group to group, the teacher can respond to any problems the students are experiencing and help them solve these problems.

3. During rehearsals, when the teacher is working with one group, the other groups can either work independently or two groups can perform for each other.

4. Students do not have a lot of lines to learn; therefore, they have more time to work on pronunciation, characterization, and body language.

5. Because most of the rehearsals take place during class time, students do not need to give up a lot of time outside class for extra rehearsals.

6. Because students are working in small groups, if one student is absent, this only affects one group and not the whole class.

## Pros of a large-scale performance

1. Students have a lot of language input when working with a long text.

2. Students have a large time commitment with possible extra rehearsals in the evenings or on weekends and therefore have more opportunities to speak in the second language with the teacher and classmates.

3. The teacher has a better overview of each student's progress in rehearsals.

4. After the performance, students feel they have achieved something really great beyond what is normally accomplished in their classes.

## Pros of both types of performance

1. Students have the opportunity to interact with different kinds of people, outside the framework of the classroom, when looking for props, scenery, and costumes and when advertising the upcoming performance.

2. Students work closely with the teacher on pronunciation and other aspects of acting during rehearsals, thus they receive a lot of one-on-one language coaching from the teacher.

## Further benefits of taking on a role

In our drama courses, we strongly encourage our students to perform at the end of the course. Even though some of our students find the prospect of acting in front of an audience frightening, we assure them that it is a fun experience and that anyone can do it even within a short period of time with some hard work and self-confidence. Many of our students would like to pursue undergraduate or graduate degrees at universities in the country of the second language. In some of their courses they may be required to give oral presentations and when they finish their course of study, to take oral exams in the second language. Acting in front of an audience in a second language is very good preparation for a student's future academic experience. In addition, many of our students hope to work for international companies or want to use the second language in their jobs, so any experience they have speaking that language in front of an audience can help them overcome their shyness and fear of using the second language in many contexts.

We have also found that many of our shyest students have really come out of themselves during rehearsals. Taking a role has boosted their confidence and made them more adventurous when conversing with native speakers. (See the Introduction for a longer list of benefits of taking a drama course.)

## Step 2: Smaller Decisions

After you have made the big decision and before starting rehearsals, you need to make some smaller decisions about the practical logistics of your performance, such as:

1. Who will the audience be?
2. How will colleagues be involved?
3. Where and when will the performance(s) be?
4. How many performances will there be?
5. What kind of performance style will be used?

## Who is your audience?

Here are three possible audiences:

- Your students perform for other classes in your program, in their own classrooms, with the permission of the teacher, and go from class to class taking the show "on the road."

- Your students perform for a larger audience made up of a number of classes from the second language program in an auditorium or other large space.
- Your students perform in their own classroom and the performance is videotaped. If they wish, they can show the videotape at a later date to an audience.

## How to involve colleagues

We like to work with colleagues when we put on a performance. As soon as we know which text or texts we will work with, we give a copy to interested colleagues so that they can read the text(s) with their classes before seeing the performance. We offer to come into our colleagues' classes before the performance with as many actors as possible to talk about how we prepared for the performance. To prepare for our visit, our colleagues ask their students to read the play as homework, to write questions about character or plot interpretation, as well as about how the actors will portray certain characters in the text. A question-and-answer session is a useful language exercise for the actors and the students in our colleagues' classes.

## Where and when to perform

Once you know who your audience is, then you need to begin to investigate what type of performance space would accommodate the audience you have chosen. You may not have a great deal of choice.

**Rooms available to you** If your students take their performance to different classes, or invite an audience to their own class, you do not need to book another room for the performance. If you want to use a different room—for example. an auditorium— we advise you to book it early, not only for the performance day(s), but also for a few rehearsals in the week before the performance. You may have to schedule an evening performance if the room is occupied during the day.

Here are the types of rooms that we have used in the past:

- Classroom type I: a not very large, flat space with movable desks

- Classroom type II: a small auditorium with fixed stadium seats, seating 40–50 students
- Large auditorium: an auditorium with a sloping floor and 100–300 fixed seats. There may or may not be a raised stage at the front.
- Lounge area: a large lounge with movable armchairs. We performed in a small area at one end of the lounge and arranged stackable plastic chairs and armchairs in rows facing the performance area. It created an intimate atmosphere between the audience and the actors.

**How the room affects the performance** Make sure you look at the room carefully before performance day and consider the following:

- Acoustics: You are familiar with your students' speaking abilities. Small rooms are better for small voices. *Remember:* The larger the room, the more your students will have to project their voices. If you don't have time to work on projection, choose a small space. To check the acoustics, speak first in a loud voice and then in a soft voice. If your voice does not reverberate, you can be sure that the audience will not hear your soft-spoken students.
- Furniture: What furniture is in the room? Can you make use of it or push it aside?
- Arrangement: Where in the room will the actors be? Where will the audience sit? We suggest that you decide early where the student actors will enter and exit the performance space. If the room has a door near the performance space, you can use that. If there is no door that you can use easily, you could have the actors stand to the side of the performance space or the audience. (See Figure 4–1 for two possible room arrangements.)

**When to perform** In a seven-week drama course, when we meet our students one hour a day, five days a week, we usually perform early in the seventh week. Week 7 in our language program is exam week. We find that staging a performance early in

Figure 4–1: Room Arrangement

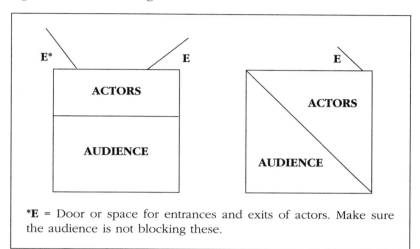

**\*E** = Door or space for entrances and exits of actors. Make sure the audience is not blocking these.

exam week distracts the actors and audience from the approaching exams. Many teachers find it hard to do much "serious" work in week 7 as the students only want to prepare for the exams or relax, so watching a performance by their colleagues provides a fun listening activity for students in other classes of the language program.

If we are taking the performance from one class to another, we usually visit classes that meet at the same time as our drama course so that the actors do not have to be excused from other classes in order to perform.

## The number of performances

For both small-scale and large-scale performances you have the option of performing one time only or more than once. If you choose one performance, it is very exciting for the students because it is their only chance to give it their all. The disadvantage of this choice is that students might feel disappointed once the performance is over—all that hard work for only one hour on stage? (This sense of disappointment can be overcome to some extent by videotaping the performance.)

If you have a number of performances of the same piece(s), students can make changes after each performance. We have found, in this case, that each performance has been very different and our students have become more relaxed after each one. Once, at a final performance in a sequence, our students were improvising their lines and actions and were thoroughly enjoying themselves. The audience sensed this and really entered into the spirit of it by cheering, whistling, and clapping.

## Performance style

You and your students will also need to decide how you are going to perform. Will you perform in a traditional manner with actors saying their lines in character, wearing costumes, on a stage? Or will the students take the text onto the stage and read the lines to the audience? If this is your first attempt at using drama, keep it simple. Here are some different performance styles for you to discuss with your students.

**Reader's theater** Reader's theater needs less preparation than a traditional-style performance because it does not require scenery or a long list of props and only a suggestion of a costume (a hat, a shawl, a pipe, or a pair of glasses). For reader's theater, the actors do thorough character studies and memorize their lines, but they do not move about the stage. They sit at desks or stand behind music stands with scripts in front of them. The effect is just as dramatic as a fully staged, costumed performance because the students say their lines in character, which holds the audience's attention and creates dramatic tension.

**Narrator and actors** A narrator can be used to introduce the play and link scenes together. If you have edited a play to make it shorter, this can help the audience understand the action better. A narrator describes in a sentence or two the parts of the story that were left out. The narrator can also facilitate a smooth transition between scenes while the stage is being prepared for the next scene.

**Puppets** If students feel shy about acting in front of an audience, using puppets is a good alternative. Different types of puppets are finger, shadow, sock, paper, or traditional wooden puppets. Depending on the type of puppets you use, they can be operated by slipping your hand into the puppet or using strings to operate it. If any students do not feel comfortable speaking before an audience, they can operate the puppets while other students talk for the puppets. These puppet operators will still have to listen carefully to the dialogue and follow along in the text so that they do not miss their cues to move the puppets.

**Music and sound effects** Using music or sound effects can help create a particular atmosphere in your performance. For example, in a scene depicting a romantic dinner for two, you could play romantic music to help set the scene. Or, you could use the sound of a thunderstorm to create an ominous or frightening mood. Our experience has been that music and sound effects often make the audience laugh. One of our groups adapted a chilling story, "The Monkey's Paw" by W. W. Jacobs. A live pianist played dramatically at the beginning of the performance and between scenes. In addition, there were sound effects to create a frightening atmosphere. During rehearsals, students were very impressed by the dramatic effect they had created and were convinced that the audience would be very frightened. However, when performance day arrived, the audience laughed whenever they heard the music or sound effects. They were too dramatic, which turned the horror story into a very funny melodrama. The performance was a great hit, but it did not quite have the effect that the actors had originally intended.

If you decide to incorporate music or sound effects, keep it simple. In addition, make sure that early on in rehearsals you work with the music or sound effects to avoid any problems on performance day: a faulty tape player, a cassette in the wrong position, incorrect volume setting, and so on.

**Dance** In one of our performances we included a short choreographed dance sequence. This was very entertaining for the audience and the actors, but it required quite a lot of rehearsal time. It can be a fun addition to a performance, but if your time is limited, we would advise against it, especially as rehearsing the dance does not lend itself to language interaction beyond a few oral instructions.

# Text work

In this section, we will take you through exercises to familiarize the students with basic theater terms, through reading and analyzing the play, assigning roles, and memorizing lines. Unless stated otherwise, we are referring to both small-scale and large-scale performances.

## Step 3: Basic Theater Terms and Text Format

Before asking the students to read the play, we like to go over some basic theater terms and discuss the format of dramatic texts with our students. We have been surprised that some of our students are not familiar with the format of a dramatic text and are not sure which parts are to be said and which are not. Once we had a student who had never seen a play script before and when it was his turn, he read, left to right, his character's name, the stage directions, *and* his lines! Here are three exercises that will help you and your students examine the meaning of theater terms and look at the format of a dramatic text.

## Exercise: Basic terms for talking about the theater and dramatic literature

**Preparation:** Make enough copies of the handout for the class (see Appendix 1: "Theater Terms" for a copy of the handout).

**Procedure:** Give your students the handout. Ask them, in pairs or small groups, to discuss the meaning of the theater terms on the handout. Then, as a whole class, discuss the meaning of the terms together. Write the definitions on the blackboard and ask the students to copy the definitions onto their handouts. As homework, tell students to review the theater terms, which they will need to know for a game in the next class.

## Exercise: Review of theater terms

**Preparation:** On individual cards or slips of paper, write one theater term from the handout (see Appendix 1: "Theater Terms") and put them in an envelope. Bring a stopwatch to class if you have one or a watch with a second hand.

**Procedure:** Put the students into two teams. One person from Team A takes one card out of the envelope. That student looks at the term, but must not show it to the other members of Team A nor tell them what is on the card. The student defines the term for Team A without saying any of the words written on the card. The other students in Team A must guess which theater term is being described. Allocate two points if Team A can guess within thirty seconds and one point if they can guess within one minute. If Team A cannot guess the correct answer after one minute, Team B is allowed to guess and wins one point for a correct answer. Next, a student from Team B takes a card from the envelope and the whole procedure is repeated, alternating between each team. The team with the most points wins.

## Exercise: Text format

**Preparation:** Make enough copies of the play for the whole class. Write the following questions on the blackboard or on an overhead projector transparency before class.

- Why are the names of the characters on the left-hand side of the page? Does the actor have to memorize and say these words?
- Where are the stage directions? Does the actor have to memorize and say these?
- Which words does the actor have to memorize and say? How are these words separated from the stage directions?

**Procedure:** Give each student a copy of the text. Ask the students, in pairs, to discuss the preceding questions concerning the format of the text.

## Step 4: General Read-through

In a general read-through, your students have the opportunity to read the text out loud and hear the words of the speakers. At this stage, they can begin to explore characters and surface meaning in the text. We suggest that you ask students to read the text at home at least once before conducting a general read-through in class. The first exercise is for a class doing several short plays and the second is for a class doing one longer play. We offer an alternative third exercise that is designed for language learners who need group practice and are going to perform short skits. As you go through the text with your students, ask them the meaning of words you think they may not know. Also, let the students ask you the meanings of words that are very important to the overall meaning of the text. Students can also look up a lot of vocabulary at home.

## Exercise 1: Read-aloud (groups: several short plays)

**Preparation:** Make sure all students have copies of the texts they will be working with.
**Procedure:** Break the class up into groups. If there are two characters in the skit or scene, break the class into pairs; if there are three characters, break the class into groups of three, and so on. If there are many parts, you can put the students into groups of any number you like and students can read more than one part. The teacher moves from group to group listening to the students read (this gives you an opportunity to see how individuals read, as well as seeing whether students are confident reading lines out loud).

## Exercise 2: Read-aloud (whole class: one full-length play)

**Preparation:** Make sure each student has a copy of the text.
**Procedure:** Sit in a circle and begin reading the play. You can either ask for volunteers to read parts or you can randomly assign roles to the students. It is important to rotate the roles frequently so that everyone has a chance to read many parts and also you can listen for which part seems to fit which student.

Each day read part of the play and answer any questions students may have as you go along. Give students a chance to discuss the plot and characters.

## Exercise 3: Read-aloud (choral, for all types of plays)

Some students need more help with a read-aloud. Here is an exercise to help them:

In a choral read-aloud, the teacher models each sentence so that the whole class, speaking as one voice, can mimic the phrasing. This is a nonthreatening exercise that allows our students to hear the script but does not require any student to speak alone in front of the class.

**Preparation:** Make enough copies of the text for the whole class.
**Procedure:** The teacher models each line of the play, asking students to listen carefully and then repeat as they try to match tempo and pitch. The teacher begins by slowly and precisely articulating each word. The class repeats slowly. The teacher then reads the same line at a faster rate with more colloquial pronunciation. Whenever there is a stumbling in the repetition, the teacher may then break the sentence into logical phrases. She may start with the end phrase, building up phrase by phrase until the class can repeat the whole set of phrases without a garbled line. For example, if the teacher wants the students to say the line, "The tiny spark of what I used to be" (from *Fortitude* by Kurt Vonnegut), she would proceed as follows:

*Teacher:* Repeat after me: Used to be.

*Students (in chorus):* Used to be.

*Teacher:* Used to be [faster].

*Students (in chorus):* Used to be.

*Teacher:* Of what I used to be [slower].

*Students (in chorus):* Of what I used to be.

*Teacher:* Of what I used to be [faster].

*Students (in chorus):* Of what I used to be.

*Teacher:* The tiny spark of what I used to be [slower].

*Students (in chorus):* The tiny spark of what I used to be.

*Teacher:* The tiny spark of what I used to be [faster].

*Students (in chorus):* The tiny spark of what I used to be.

You can break the phrase into as many segments as you like and you can practice it many times until you feel the students are comfortable with it.

## Step 5: Text Analysis

Next, you and your students can start interpreting the play. Text analysis allows the students to explore what is happening in the text, to whom it is happening, and why. We usually divide this stage into a general analysis concentrating on surface aspects of the text and an in-depth analysis where students try to understand the deeper meaning of the text.

If you are conducting a large-scale performance, divide the class into groups and give each group a different scene to work on. If you are doing a small-scale performance, give each group a different skit to work on.

## General text analysis

### Exercise: general meaning

**Preparation:** Write the following on the blackboard or on an overhead transparency:

- Who are the characters and what do they do in the text?
- What are the most important events in the text?
- What is the mood? Funny? Sad?

**Procedure:** Ask the students to discuss the above questions in pairs for a couple of minutes. Then, share the answers as a whole class.

## In-depth text analysis

At this stage, students delve a little deeper into the whys and wherefores of the text instead of looking only at the plot and characters at a superficial level. We ask the students to go below the meaning of the words and phrases in the text and, like professional actors, look for the *subtext*. You might guess from the word "subtext" that actors look for something *not* said, some meaning underlying the words.

By examining possible subtext and imagining the reasons why characters say what they do, students can better understand what is happening, where it is happening, who is involved in the action, what the relationships between the characters are, and why the action is happening.

Here are some exercises to help you and your students explore the text in more depth:

### Exercise: text analysis for plot and character

**Preparation:** Prepare questions for each skit that you will use in this exercise and place these questions on a handout.

Here are two sections from *Nosey Busy Body* (see Appendix 2) with the kinds of questions that we think bring out good discussion.

### Section 1 of *Nosey Busy Body*

*B:* What's the matter?

*A:* Oh, nothing . . .

*B:* What do you mean, "Oh, nothing . . ."? It doesn't sound like nothing to me.

*A:* I don't want to talk about it.

*B:* (*hurt*) Oh, OK. (*pause*) Why not?

*A:* Because I just don't. That's why.

*B:* Oooooooh. Sorry. I just wanted to help.

### Questions for Section 1

- What do you know about A and B?
- Are there any clues about A and B's ages?
- Are there any clues about A and B's relationship?
- What does the title mean?
- Which character is the nosey busy body?
- What doesn't A want to talk about or aren't we told yet?
- What do you think is meant by the three periods after "Oh, nothing . . ."?
- What kind of information goes in between the parentheses ( )?

### Section 2 of *Nosey Busy Body*

*A:* (*Deciding to take a chance*) Have you noticed anything about Elliott lately?

*B:* No. (*A little worried*) What could I have noticed?

*A:* Surely you've seen how strange he's been acting?

*B:* Strange? What do you mean?

*A:* He's been so secretive. I mean, for example, last night...

*B:* (*jumping up*) What about last night?

*A:* Well, he wouldn't say when he was coming home from work. First, he had told me, "Not until nine." Then he called at eight-thirty and said that he wouldn't be finished and couldn't get home till after ten-thirty. Wouldn't you wonder? (*Suddenly blurts out*) You don't think he's having an affair, do you?

Questions for Section 2:
- How is this section different from the first section?
- Do you think A and B trust each other?
- What do you think Elliott was doing last night?
- What do you think B was doing last night?
- Why is A confiding in B?

**Procedure:** Divide the class into small groups. Each group gets a handout with questions about one scene from the play. Ask the students to discuss the questions regarding the plot and characters in the scene they have been assigned. After the students have discussed these questions, ask them to join with another group to discuss their scene or skit. Next, as a whole group, students share their ideas about the plot and characters in the play.

## Exercise: text analysis for setting and time
**Preparation:** Write the following questions on the blackboard or on an overhead transparency:

- In what country does the action happen? Does it matter?
- Where are the characters from?
- Where specifically does the action take place? In someone's home? In a public place? Out-of-doors?
- In which century or time period does the action happen? The eighteenth century? In the 1960s? In the future?
- Does the action take place during the day? At night? What difference would it make if the play happened at a different time and place from how you imagine?

**Procedure:** In small groups, ask the students to discuss the preceding questions with reference to their scene and report back to the rest of the class when they have finished.

## Exercise: text analysis for plot

**Preparation:** Write the following questions on the blackboard or on an overhead transparency:

- What happened just before the scene began?
- What is the general idea of the scene? (What happens to whom?)
- What do you predict will happen just after the last lines of the scene?

**Procedure:** In small groups the students discuss the preceding questions. Then, ask the students, in groups, to prepare a short (one-minute) performance related to their scene, but in their own words. They can choose to condense all the action of the scene into a one-minute summary and act that out; they can act out the scene immediately before theirs began; or they can act out the scene immediately after theirs finished. Once they have practiced their scene, ask the students to perform it for the class.

## Exercise: text analysis for character

We often ask students to write a character biography to help them explore one character in more depth. In a character biography, we look for what the playwright tells us about that character: physical appearance, childhood, family, education, work history, love life, hopes, likes and dislikes, or problems from four main sources: the character's own words, the words of other characters, the subtext, and the stage directions.

**Preparation:** Make enough copies of the worksheet for each pair in the class (see Appendix 1: "Character Biography" for a copy of the worksheet).

**Procedure:** Divide the class into pairs. Give each pair a different scene and ask the students to fill in the worksheet referring only to their scene. Tell them to start by using any clues in the dialog that give any information about the character's physical appearance, color of hair or eyes, comparative height or weight to other characters, any outstanding facial feature, or the comparative youth or age to other characters. Are there references to the character's personality? What adjectives have been used in describing the character? To do this, the pair needs to look carefully at every line of their scene. The students must fill in the worksheet as if they were that character. When the students have filled in their worksheets, ask them to compare their answers with another group.

## Step 6: Assigning Roles

Before we assign roles to our students, we emphasize the fact that everybody will be working as a team and no one, no matter how large or small the role, is more or less important than the other. We also tell our students that those who do not have a large role will have the opportunity to take one or two smaller roles if they like, or they can assist the director, or they can be responsible for a number of backstage jobs (these are described in step 15). When dividing roles, you have to ensure that your students are given a chance to say which role they want to play. They will be more motivated to put in their best effort if they are playing a role they actually want.

### Method for assigning roles

**Method 1:**

1. We write all the roles in the play on the blackboard or in a notebook. Next to each character's name we write whether this is a female, male, or neutral role—that is, if it can be played by a man or a woman.

2. We go through each role in turn with the whole class and ask for volunteers to play the roles. We keep track of who wants each role in our notebook or on the blackboard.

3. If more than one student would like to play a role, we let those students audition in front of their classmates. They read a few lines from the role to the whole class and their classmates vote on which person they like best for the role.

**Method 2** Alternatively, we draw names to decide who plays the role. Choose the method that you think is the fairest for your students. The last thing you want is to have students with hurt feelings, so keep emphasizing the fact that everyone's role in the production is equally important.

## Should the teacher take a role?

We advise teachers not to take a role in the performance. We see our role as director, helper, and advisor. We need to be available during rehearsals to help students with the language and various aspects of acting. We have taken on roles in the past; for example, if a student was absent for a performance, we jumped in. We once had a very small class made up of three students. In that case, we were forced to take on a couple of roles. However, we were working as one group, so we were able to guide our students through any problems they faced in preparing their roles.

### Step 7: In-depth Read-through

## Meaning revisited

### Small-scale: when a class performs several short plays

1. In groups, students read the play out loud, reading the roles assigned to them. They should read the play aloud twice to remind them about what happens and to become familiar with the voices of the other actors.

2. Students discuss what is happening, when it is happening, where it is happening, why it is happening, who is involved in the action, and what the relationships are between the different characters.

Give each group a production book to use during rehearsals. In this book, students can summarize what they did in rehearsals and they can jot down questions or problems and make a note of what they want to work on in their next rehearsal. In addition, they can use the book to summarize the most important points of group discussions. Each member of the group, in turn, is responsible for writing in the production book. The writer for each rehearsal not only has to participate in the rehearsal as an active member of the group, but also has to listen and watch attentively, summarize the main issues or questions, then record them in the book. These are crucial skills for any student or employee in any field. The teacher can collect the books at the end of each week to monitor each group's progress and to check that they have actually been using the notebook.

Tell your students that they might not be able to answer all the questions they have about plot and characters immediately and that they may disagree on some of these answers. Tell them that they will be able to solve these problems once they begin acting out the scenes. As we mentioned in the introduction to this book, when we were preparing for a performance of *Twelve Angry Jurors*, we had a student with a small role who realized how important that role was only later in the rehearsal process.

**Large-scale: when the class is involved in one long play** While sitting in a circle, students read through the play once, reading their own roles. Next, have students read through a few scenes at a time. Stop them to ask questions about plot, characters, and relationships: what is happening, to whom, and why?

## Saying the lines

The next step is for your students to practice saying the words of their characters (their lines).

**Teacher demonstration** Stand in front of the whole class and tell your students you are going to say the same sentence twice and ask them to think about what differences there are between the two sentences. Take any sentence from the play and, first of all, say it in your conversational voice (the voice you would use talking to a friend who is standing beside you). Do not use your teacher voice—that is, do not project your voice. Speak at a normal speed and do not overenunciate the words. While you are speaking, adopt a normal stance and address a student in the front row of the class.

The second time you say the sentence, stand up very straight with your shoulders back, your head up, and look out beyond the group of students to the back wall of the classroom. Speak like an actor: slow down the speed of delivery slightly so that it is slower than the pace of normal speech. Enunciate the words very clearly, pronounce the consonants at the end of the words precisely, emphasize stress slightly more than in normal speech and project your voice, so that you are speaking at a higher volume than normal (see "Projecting the Voice" in Chapter 2).

After this demonstration, discuss the following questions with your students:

- Which sentence was easier to understand?
- Which sentence was more like everyday speech? Why?
- How was the other sentence different from everyday speech?
- If you were saying this sentence to a large room full of people, which way of saying it would be better? Why?
- Did my body language change when I said each sentence? How did it change? What effect did this have on the way I said the sentence?

Tell the students that when they deliver their lines in front of an audience, they have to help the audience understand what they say. In order to do this, they need to speak very clearly by pronouncing the words clearly, especially the consonants at the end of the words, and by projecting their voices and thus speaking louder and slower than normal.

**Student practice: Saying the lines** Divide the class into small groups and work with one group at a time. While you are working with one pair, have the other students say some of their lines, in turn, by enunciating the words and paying particular attention to stress and intonation. Students should listen to each other and try to understand what is being said. If they are unable to understand what a classmate says, they should work on this together by thinking about how the stress, rhythm, and intonation could be altered to better aid understanding. The teacher can move from group to group listening to students saying their lines and helping them make corrections where necessary. If a student mispronounces individual consonants or vowels to such an extent that the student's lines are incomprehensible, the teacher can work closely with the student on that problem (see the pronunciation exercises in Chapter 2 for more details). Advise students to mark their texts as they work on saying their lines by circling trouble-

some sounds and words where they miss the stress or by mark-
ing intonation patterns. For example:

allow    won't allow

Also, students can mark their texts with a dot or an asterisk to show
when to take a deep breath. They can continue to work on this
at home. As rehearsals progress, continue correcting students if it
is difficult to understand their lines.

## Student Practice: Breathing and projecting the voice
Tell your students that breathing deeply will help them relax while
performing and it will help them project their voices so that the
audience can hear them. Start with one of the relaxation exercises
in Chapter 2 and then do the "Projecting the Voice" exercise with
your students. Tell your students to practice saying their lines at
home very clearly in an actor's voice while standing up straight,
breathing deeply, and using abdominal muscles to help them
project their voices.

## Step 8: Memorizing Lines
Once students have a good grasp of what is happening in the play
and have practiced saying their lines carefully, they can begin
memorizing their lines. It is much easier to work on characterization, gestures, and body language once students have memorized
their lines and no longer need to hold the play in their hands. Here
are two ways of memorizing lines:

### Using the text
Students work with the text at home and should probably do no
more than a scene at a time. They read a section of the text two
or three times out loud, saying all the lines. Then they cover the
text, revealing only one line at a time. They read the lines of the
other characters out loud, but when they get to their own lines,
they keep them covered and try to recite these lines from memory.
For some students, a page a day might be a reasonable goal,
memorizing in this manner until they are able to say all their lines

perfectly. The next day they work in a similar manner with the next section of the text until they know all their lines in the play by heart.

Some actors use a method of writing only the first letter of each word of a line. They write out the last few words of the line just before theirs and then look at this "code" of beginning letters. (For instance, "They told me to take a streetcar named Desire . . ." would look like: T t m t t a s n D.) We usually advise students to memorize two lines at a time and in the process, they can test themselves on earlier lines that they already memorized.

## Using audiotapes

There are several methods of using the tape recorder to help students to learn their lines. One method is to record just cue lines. When trying to memorize, the students listen to the cue and then the students push the pause button while they say their own line after which they go on to the next cue. Another method is to record only the lines the students want to learn, with a few words of the line before it to cue them. This way the student can say the line with the recorded voice, repeating as often as needed.

Another way of learning lines is for students to make an audio recording of the scenes they are in. Each student records the whole scene, reading all lines including their own, onto a tape. If a student does not own a tape recorder, you can arrange for each student to take a blank tape to the language lab to record the scenes they want to work with. The students then can work with their own cassette tape in the lab in the following manner:

1. Students listen to one whole scene once without stopping the tape.

2. On the second listening of the text, the students pause the tape after the cue line and just before their own line. They say their line out loud.

3. They then listen to the line to check if they said it correctly. They work in this manner until they have memorized a set of lines. Encourage students to listen to their lines at every opportunity (walking to and from classes) so that they know their cues and lines automatically.

A variation of this method is to make a master tape of the whole play with all cast members contributing their lines (in the language laboratory), but this is sometimes difficult to arrange. The students can bring blank tapes to the lab and have the master tape speed-transferred to the student tapes.

The advantage of this last method is that each student hears the voices of the other actors giving audio cues for lines. This best simulates the actual experience of hearing the lines as the actors say them (as long as the actors do not forget their lines!). If students learn lines by only reading the text, they do not hear the actual voices of the other actors with all their particular inflections.

## Rehearsals

In Steps 9–14, we suggest exercises you can use with your students to practice different aspects of acting. We suggest you spend one or two class sessions (if you have time) concentrating on each step in the "Rehearsals" section of this chapter. We have listed a number of exercises for each step, which can be found in Chapter 2. You will not have time to do all the exercises, so choose the ones you like best. For exercises that use a text, we use parts of *Nosey Busy Body* (see Appendix 2 for the full script) to illustrate the exercise; you can adapt these exercises for whatever text you use. We suggest you start each rehearsal with a short relaxation exercise (see the first three relaxation exercises in Chapter 2). These exercises will help your students to relax and focus on the tasks in class. In addition, before getting into rehearsals, we recommend you use some of the improvisation exercises in Chapter 2. These exercises are fun and build students' confidence in their ability to get up on stage and act. The group exercises build a strong acting team (see especially Chapter 2, the improvisation exercises "News Anchor" "Group Improvisation").

The way you organize rehearsals depends on the type of performance you are planning. For a small-scale performance, the students can work on their skits in small groups. You can then rotate from group to group during class-time rehearsals. We suggest you spend at least fifteen minutes working with any group. This allows you time to help students work through any problems and you can get a better sense of how that group is progressing. While you work with one group, the other students work in their own groups.

For a large-scale performance, you will need to draw up a rehearsal schedule outlining the scenes you will rehearse during each class. Give a copy of this schedule to the students and tell them they are required to attend all rehearsals because they are held during class time. For those students who do not appear in the scenes you are rehearsing on a particular day get them to work in pairs, listening to each other's lines. One student reads the cues while looking at the text and checks that the partner says the lines correctly. These pairs can also work on other aspects of acting, such as voice and movement (see Steps 9–14 for more details).

Rehearsal time should be divided up as follows (based on a 50-minute lesson):

## Exercises (approximately 10 minutes)

- Tell students which area of acting you will concentrate on that day—for example, voice, facial expressions, or movement.
- In groups, students work through one or two exercises in the designated area of acting.

## Text work (40 minutes)

- Students work with the play and work on the area dealt with in the exercises either with you watching and guiding them, or with other students' help.

### *Step 9: Voice*

We suggest you start rehearsals on voice with two introductory exercises that examine the impression made by different kinds of voices:

- Different Voices—a Cultural Perspective (see Chapter 2)
- Different Voices—an American Perspective (see Chapter 2)

Then proceed to active exercises, where students experiment with their own voices. The following are good warm-up exercises:

- Loud and Soft Words (see Chapter 2)
- Nonsense Conversation (see Chapter 2)
- Nonsense Emotions (see Chapter 2)

These in-depth voice exercises explore the characters in the class texts:

- Voices of Characters (see Chapter 2)
- Emotions of Characters in a Text (see Chapter 2)

If your performance space is different from your classroom, we would suggest you practice voice projection with your students in the performance space so that they experience how their voices carry in the room where they will perform:

- Projecting the Voice (see Chapter 2)

## Step 10: Timing and Speed of Delivery

Timing is so important in acting—it can make all the difference between two students saying lines to each other and two believable characters having a real interaction on stage. Here is a short extract from *Nosey Busy Body* (see Appendix 2) followed by an exercise, which focuses on timing (how fast or slow lines should be delivered).

### Nosey Busy Body (Lines 10–13)

*slow*                           *fast*

A: [Surely], [you've seen how strange he's been acting.]

*fast*                           *slow*

B: [Strange?] [What do you mean?]

*slow*                                             *fast*

A: [He's been so secretive.] [I mean, for example, last night…]

*fast*

B: [(*Jumping up*) What about last night?]

## Timing exercise (with a text)

Tell the students to think about how fast to say the preceding lines and how much time to leave between words, phrases, and sentences. Tell students to think also about pauses: How long should they last? What is the difference between a long or short pause in different places in the text? We have marked some lines from *Nosey Busy Body* to get students started. Students should experiment with the speed of their lines and pauses. They can examine how the effect of the words changes if they change the speed of delivery.

### *Step 11: Facial Expressions*

This is another area that can be difficult because usually we do not see how our faces look during interaction with another person. Students need to be aware of how to create different facial expressions and how each facial expression feels physically. In addition, students will need to decide if certain expressions are appropriate for the character they are playing. The first three exercises in the following list introduce the students to making different facial expressions. The fourth exercise works with facial expressions of characters in their texts:

- Introduction (see Chapter 2)
- Emotions in the Face (see Chapter 2)
- Emotions Game (see Chapter 2)
- Facial Expressions in a Text (see Chapter 2)

### *Step 12: Gestures*

Here are three exercises for practicing gestures. The first is a warm-up exercise; in the second exercise students convey emotions through gestures; and in the third exercise students examine the gestures of characters in a text:

- Introduction to Gestures (see Chapter 2)
- Emotions in Gestures (see Chapter 2)
- Gestures in a Text (see Chapter 2)

## *Step 13: Posture*

When acting it can be hard to know how to hold the body when playing a character. Should you stand slumped over and sloppy or should you stand up very straight and tense? Students will need help with this area of acting, as they will feel self-conscious about putting their bodies into different positions. The first two exercises that follow are introductory warm-up exercises. In the last two exercises, students discuss the postures of characters in a text.

- Introduction to Postures (see Chapter 2)
- Different People, Different Postures (see Chapter 2)
- Postures of Characters in a Text (see Chapter 2)
- Postures in a Text (see Chapter 2)

## *Step 14: Movement*

Here are four golden rules concerning movement:

Rule 1: Make sure the audience can see all actors on stage, as shown:

Actor 1 (speaks)

Actor 2 (listens)                                        Actor 3 (listens)

A U D I E N C E

Rule 2: If one actor is speaking, other actors should stand still. If they walk around, they will distract the audience from what the speaker is saying.
Rule 3: If you videotape a performance, you need to be aware of the fact that the actual camera frame is quite narrow. Therefore, either the actors will have to be careful not to step outside that camera frame if the camera stays still, or the camera operator will have to follow the action with the camera during the performance.
Rule 4: Never allow an actor to say lines facing away from the audience.

Here are some exercises to help your students practice movement. The first five exercises are warm-up exercises:

- Walking Randomly (see Chapter 2)
- Walking Through Different Types of Terrain (see Chapter 2)
- Showing Emotions (see Chapter 2)
- Sculptor and Sculpture (see Chapter 2)
- Mirroring (see Chapter 2)

In the next three exercises, students observe movement and discuss issues of personal space:

- Observing Movement (see Chapter 2)
- Personal Space (see Chapter 2)
- Personal Space in Everyday Situations (see Chapter 2)

In the last exercise, students connect words in a text with movements on stage:

- Movements of Characters in a Text (see Chapter 2)

The last movement exercise shows one method of mapping out the actors' movements in a play. If you have time, you can record (or have a student record) actors' actions onto a master copy of the script. If time is limited, let students improvise and do not put too much emphasis on having fixed movements, unless you see traffic problems—students bumping into each other.

We also recommend you do some mime exercises with your students as they will probably use mime in some form in their performance. Here are four mime exercises:

- Telephoning (see Chapter 2)
- Actions in Detail (see Chapter 2)
- Driven to Distraction (see Chapter 2)
- Actions Game (see Chapter 2)

# Performance Details

## *Step 15: Preperformance Details*

### Backstage jobs

Before performance day arrives, there are a number of backstage jobs to be organized:

- Costumes
- Scenery and furniture
- Props
- Advertising
- Audiovisual equipment

We like to hold a meeting early in rehearsals to outline what needs to be done and to divide up the work. As rehearsals progress and performance day draws closer we meet again to make sure everything is organized. We divide the class into groups, so that one group is responsible for scenery, another for furniture, another for props, and so on. These groups should go through the text of the play, read stage directions, and draw up a list of what is needed for each scene. Someone from each group will have to search for and then collect the items. Later, a list should be drawn up of all props and costumes and who needs them on stage during which scene. A copy of the list should be with one designated person.

**Costumes** If students want to wear costumes, tell them to keep it simple. Students are responsible for finding their own costumes. They should start in their own closets, then in their friends' closets. If students cannot find something, they might be able to borrow or buy an item very cheaply from a second-hand store. Alternatives to costumes are small symbols to suggest a character: a hat, a moustache drawn on the face, or a pair of glasses.

**Scenery and furniture** Once again keep things simple. We try to avoid using scenery as it is yet another thing to worry about before and during a performance. At times, to hide an ugly wall, we have taped a large sheet to the back wall of whatever room we are using, or we have taped signs or pictures to a wall to suggest a particular setting. As far as furniture is concerned, we try to make do with the furniture available in the room we are using. Remember, if you want to change the furniture arrangement from one scene to another, someone has to carry the furniture on and off stage between scenes. If we do change the furniture arrangement, the actors leaving a scene set up the furniture for the actors in the next scene.

**Props** Finding props can become a time-consuming burden and so we try to eliminate them as much as possible. It is best to keep it very simple. If we can teach our students to mime action well (for example, drinking a cup of coffee) they do not need to have any objects on stage to depict that action. Sometimes using a prop is distracting to students and they lose focus. Make sure you include all props early in rehearsals to see if they help or hinder the students. If students can use the props easily, fine, however, if the acting becomes awkward or difficult because of a prop, abandon it.

If students insist on having props, you might consider having them make their own. For the show about the Titanic, students made marvelous props out of cardboard and paper: an axe made of heavy paper and aluminum foil, and the sea represented by a blue sheet stretched across the front of the stage.

**Advertising** We would suggest you begin to advertise your performance about two weeks in advance. Students can do this in a number of ways: posters, email messages to teachers asking them to announce the performance to their students, word-of-mouth: the actors tell their friends to come.

**Audiovisual equipment** We often videotape our students' performances and put a master copy in the video/audio lab so that students can record it for themselves.

Where to get the equipment?
- The local public library has a video camera that various groups or individuals may borrow. We videotaped the performance with our students or us operating the camera.
- We have also used a free service from the university's technical support department that provides a camera and an operator.

This has always worked really well as we have not had to worry about the logistics of operating the camera.

- Our own department has purchased a video camera for the Intensive English Programs to use.

*Before taping* If you decide to operate the camera yourself or you get a student to do the videotaping, you need to practice using the camera before performance day. We suggest you film part of a rehearsal in the space you will use on performance day and then watch the recording to check for quality. On performance day, you will need to make sure the batteries and the spares are charged if you are using a handheld camera. If the camera is plugged into the wall, make sure you have access to an extension lead if necessary.

*Setting up camera shots* If you are videotaping a live performance in an auditorium with an audience, the camera operator will not be able to walk around during the performance. The best place to set up the camera is on a tripod at one side of the audience or behind the audience (remember the audience will not be able to see if they are sitting directly behind the camera). In a small room, the camera can be set up directly behind the audience. It is easiest for the operator if the camera is set up so that the whole stage can be seen through the lens, then the operator does not have to continually look through the lens during the performance and move the camera to follow the actors.

If you are not performing for a live audience, but are taping in class, you have more flexibility. You can set the camera on a tripod at the back of the room, but the operator can also move the camera to follow the action and zoom in or out to focus on particular characters. We would suggest that you film scene by scene and stop between scenes to review the recording. If students do not like their performance, you can film the scene again. This method of filming will take much longer than simply letting the camera record while the whole performance runs through once, so you will need to either build this into your class time or find time outside class.

## Jobs on performance day

- Welcome, introductions, and thanks by master of ceremonies
- Prompter

- Changing scenery/arranging furniture and props
- Audiovisual equipment operator

**Welcome, introductions, and thanks by master of ceremonies** Before a performance begins, one of our students welcomes the audience, introduces the actors, and thanks anyone who helped the students to prepare for the performance. Make a running list of all the people who helped you prepare for your performance as you go along, then you will not be in danger of forgetting to mention anyone at the performance.

**Prompter** A prompter silently reads the text as the actors are saying their lines. The prompter tells the actors their lines if they forget them during the performance. We have prompted ourselves or we have used students with smaller roles to prompt. Whoever you use, make sure the prompter practices during rehearsals and knows what to do on performance day. He or she can do this by prompting during rehearsals: if an actor forgets a line, he or she should say, "cue" so that the prompter can clearly say the line to the actor. The best place for the prompter to sit during a performance is in the center seat of the front row directly in front of the stage (reserve this seat).

**Changing scenery/arranging furniture and props** If scenery or furniture needs to be changed between scenes, we have the outgoing actors arrange this for the actors in the next scene. As regards props, all props are placed on a table in the wings on each side of the stage before the performance begins. All actors are responsible for checking that everything they need is on the table before they go on stage. Actors carry their props onto stage with them and place them back on the table when they come off stage.

**Audiovisual equipment operator** If you are using audiovisual equipment, make sure you know who will operate it before performance day. Also, the equipment operator should practice using this equipment before performance day.

### Step 16: Postperformance

We like to meet our students at least once after the performance to talk about how it went. We ask them the following questions:

1. How do you think the performance went?
2. Were there any problems? How were they solved?
3. How would you change the performance if you could do it one more time?
4. What did you learn from acting in a play?

In addition to the postperformance autopsy, we like to have a postperformance party where we watch the video of the performance, swap addresses, and have fun! In this book, we have given you the tools to facilitate your students' gaining fluency. We have described how to set up a drama class so that you create a comfortable and productive learning environment. We have provided exercises to set up the atmosphere in the class and to work on various aspects of acting. We have offered suggestions about where to find texts, how to adapt them to suit your students, and how to guide your students through writing their own texts. Finally, we have taken you stage by stage through the rehearsal process to performance day. The rest is now up to you and your students. Break a leg!

# Appendix 1

## Teaching Handouts

### Theater Terms

Write a definition of the following terms:

COMEDY _____

TRAGEDY _____

SOAP OPERA _____

MELODRAMA _____

CHARACTER _____

DIALOG _____

PLOT _____

STAGE DIRECTIONS _____

CUE _____

WINGS _____

SCENERY/SET _____

PROPS _____

COSTUMES _____

HERO/HEROINE _____

VILLAIN _____

BREAK A LEG _____

# Theater Terms (definitions)

| | |
|---|---|
| COMEDY | A story that is funny. |
| TRAGEDY | A story in which at least one character dies. |
| SOAP OPERA | A story that is very easy to follow and is exaggerated. In the story many shocking events happen to the people involved. These are very popular on television. |
| MELODRAMA | A serious story acted in an exaggerated manner so that it is funny. |
| CHARACTER | A person in the play. |
| DIALOGUE | The words people say in the play. |
| PLOT | The story in the play. |
| STAGE DIRECTIONS | The playwright gives directions to the actors about how to say lines and when and where to move. The playwright also describes the scenery in the play. |
| CUE | The last words of the previous actor's speech. Also, a signal for action, such as lighting cue or sound cue. |
| WINGS | The space offstage to the right or left of the stage. |
| SCENERY / SET | Anything used to denote location, i.e., doors, windows, furniture, etc. |
| PROPS | The objects actors use on stage to help them create a scene or a character—for example a real cup and saucer, an umbrella. |
| COSTUMES | The clothes actors wear on stage. |
| HERO/HEROINE | The main male/female people in a play. They are usually good. |
| VILLAIN | This is the evil person who tries to do harm to the hero or heroine. |
| BREAK A LEG | A theater term meaning GOOD LUCK. It is BAD luck to say "Good luck" to an actor before a performance. |

## Character Biography

I am _____ (name)

I am a _____ male _____ female

I am ___tall___ short____ skinny___overweight ___I don't know

I am _____ (approximate age)

I am _____ single_____ married_____divorced_____widowed

My husband/wife is_____(name)

My children are_____ (names)

My background: place of birth, nationality, education, family ___

_____

My work: _____

_____

My relationships to the following people: do I like/dislike them?

Character 1: _____

Character 2: _____

Character 3: _____

Character 4: _____

What do I care about in this play (scene)?

# Appendix 2

## Scripts

### Nosey Busy Body

*B:* What's the matter?

*A:* Oh, nothing. . . .

*B:* What do you mean, "Oh, nothing. . . . "? It doesn't sound like nothing to me.

*A:* I don't want to talk about it.

*B:* (*hurt*) Oh, OK. (*pause*) Why not?

*A:* Because I just don't. That's why.

*B:* Oooooooh. Sorry. I just wanted to help.

*A:* (*Deciding to take a chance*) Have you noticed anything about Elliott lately?

*B:* No. (*A little worried*) What could I have noticed?

*A:* Surely you've seen how strange he's been acting?

*B:* Strange? What do you mean?

*A:* He's been so secretive. I mean, for example, last night. . . .

*B:* (*Jumping up*) What about last night?

*A:* Well, he wouldn't say when he was coming home from work. First, he had told me, "Not until nine." Then he called at eight-thirty and said that he wouldn't be finished and couldn't get home till after ten-thirty. Wouldn't you wonder? (*Suddenly blurts out*) You don't think he's having an affair, do you?

*B:* (*A little relieved*) (*sits down*) No! There's nothing to worry about. He's such a good guy. So loyal, so trustworthy.

A:   (*A little suspicious*) How can *you* be so sure?

B:   Oh, come on. I've known you both for years. You're the ideal couple. Everyone thinks of you as the model of the happily married!

A:   Well, I don't exactly feel like half of the happily married anything now.

B:   (*Solicitous again*) Why? What's the matter? You've got to tell someone and we're best friends. You'll feel better, honestly.

A:   (*Remains silent, looking at her "best friend"*)

B    Why were you so worried when I asked you about last night?

A:   Elliott never comes home late—and if he does, I know about it days before, and why. He's just not a spontaneous person!

B:   (*Laughs*) Yes. He certainly is a good planner.

A:   What are you laughing at?

B:   Oh, nothing.

A:   Oh, do share the joke! I'm your best friend, remember?

B:   (*Trying to soothe A*) I'm sure that he had a good reason.

A:   Do you know more about this than you're telling me?

B:   Don't be ridiculous!

A:   (*On the attack now*) You look guilty. Why are you blushing?

B:   I'm not blushing! You're imagining things. I'm just warm. Isn't it warm in here? I'll open a window! (*Jumps up and goes to the window*)

A:   If you know something, you should tell me.

B:   Noo. . . . only. . . . I'm not supposed to say anything to you about this. I promised to keep my mouth shut. OK, OK. But don't tell Elliott I told you. (*She takes a deep breath, trying to think of what to say*) He, he called Richard last night. He's . . . He's . . . having some problems at work.

A:   (*Shocked*) What kind of problems?

B:   Oh, you know . . . work problems. (*B looks at watch*)

A:   Why did he ring Richard? He hardly knows him.

B:   Well, you know, this, um, client knows Richard and well, obviously he thought he could help if he told Richard and then Richard told me because, because . . .

*A:* What's the matter with you? You're fumbling; you're hiding something! And why do you keep looking at your watch?

*B:* No, I'm not. Well, yes. I am. I have to call Ellio oh-oh—I mean Richard. I mean I've got to leave. . . .

*A:* Did you say Elliott?

*B:* Elliott? Did I say Elliott? Of course, I meant Richard. We were just talking about Elliott; that's why it slipped out. . . .

*A:* What's going on between you two? I knew there was something fishy!

*B:* Yes. Yes, you're right. There's this woman at work and she won't leave him alone. He's tried everything he can to show her he's not interested. But, but she's incorrigible!

*A:* I knew it! I knew it! But, . . . what have you got to do with it?

*B:* Well, he—Elliott—he told me about it. He didn't know whether to tell you—(*checking her watch one more time*)—so he asked me for *HELP*!!! (*Door bursts open. Elliott and others come in wearing party hats, blowing horns, and carrying a birthday cake*)

*All:* Surprise!!!

## Pocket Watch

*Scene:*   (*Just outside a professor's office in the hallway of a large building. There are two students waiting to see the professor.*)

*Tracy:*   I just love this course. (*Chewing gum*)

*Corey:*   Which class is it?

*Tracy:*   The 340, the one at two o'clock.

*Corey:*   Oh yes. I remember. I liked it, too, and I came out with an A.

*Tracy:*   No kidding?

*Corey:*   Does he still put his pocket watch on the lectern before he gives his lecture? I remember he always stopped the class at exactly two forty-nine, picked up his watch and put it in his pocket, and after gathering up his notes, walked out very fast.

*Tracy:*   Oh, yeah, you're right, he does do that. Isn't it funny?

*Corey:*   But he's really a good teacher. It's because I wanted to take that course that I decided to study in Florence the summer before.

*Tracy:*   What country is Florence in? Is it France? France is great! All those pictures—so cool! And the sculpture! The artists really knew about life, didn't they? I'm an artist, too, you know.

*Corey:*   No. Well . . . what do you work in?

*Tracy:*   Pardon me? You mean, like, clothes?

*Corey:*   No. I mean, you know, like watercolors, oils . . . sculpting plasticene?

*Tracy:*   Oh, yeah. I'm like, still searching.

*Corey:*   You are? Well, tell me when you get there.

*Tracy:*   Sure thing! But I've got to get past this course's paper. I sure wish this prof would show up. I've got a lunch date.

*Corey:*   I'm sure you do.

*Tracy:*   I've been trying to write this paper for weeks, but I'm not sure if it's an A paper yet. You said that you're an art history major?

| | |
|---|---|
| *Corey:* | Yes. |
| *Tracy:* | That's so cool. Would you, like, be willing to take a quick peek at what I've written? I mean, here we are, both of us just waiting. And, like you said, you're an art history major; you really know the subject. |
| *Corey:* | Well, I suppose I could look it over. I take it you have it with you. |
| *Tracy:* | Here. (*She digs in her book bag. Pulls out one page, then another, and finally all the paper.*) |
| *Corey:* | (*He takes it and after shuffling the pages around, getting it in order, starts to read.*) Hmm! This looks really good! Quite detailed. (*He reads on.*) This part. . . . where did you get the information? |
| *Tracy:* | (*She looks at where he points.*) That part? For sure it was in that book in the library. I spent hours poring over all kinds of books. Lots of them. This part must be from one of them; yeah, probably the big oversized one with all the pictures. |
| *Corey:* | I didn't know the library had anything on that particular Italian painter. |
| *Tracy:* | Italian? I thought from his name he was French. |
| *Corey:* | But you wrote that he was a major influence on the later Italian painters who studied with him. His studio was in Florence, Italy. |
| *Tracy:* | Oh, yeah. I forgot that part. |
| *Corey:* | You're really lucky to run into me, you know. I wrote a paper for that class and it just happens that I wrote about the same painter. |
| *Tracy:* | Wow! Really? So, you know everything about him? |
| *Corey:* | Well, I wouldn't go so far as to say that. |
| *Tracy:* | Oh. Could you help me? I've just gotta get an A. |
| *Corey:* | From what I see here, you don't need anything else. It got me an A when I wrote it six months ago! |
| *Tracy:* | Hey, wait a minute! Are you accusing me of stealing this stuff? |

*Corey:* Well, the language looks very familiar. How did you get hold of this paper?

*Tracy:* I can't believe this. This is so stupid. I would never . . . Oh, there's Professor _____ now.

*Corey:* Good! Let's talk to him about this little problem.

*Tracy:* Don't you dare! That's, like, so mean! We can work this out without him. . . . (*The professor comes to a halt. Snaps his fingers*)

*Professor:* I left my watch on the podium. (*He pulls out his pocket watch from its little pocket. Looks at it. Puts it back in the pocket.*) AND I DON'T HAVE TIME TO GO BACK FOR IT!

(*The professor turns on his heels and leaves. The students' mouths drop open; they are speechless!*)

# The Wallet

*Scene 1*

(*A young man enters, speaking into a cell phone. He squints at a wallet in his hand. He is in the lobby of a hotel—we can see the letters SHERATON.*)

*Rob:* What's his name again? No, I can't read without them. I couldn't find them when I was getting ready to leave. . . . I know, I know, a place for everything and everything in its place. They are somewhere in my room, but I didn't have time to look for them before I left. (*He listens.*) Sure I will—as soon as I get this wallet back to its rightful owner. I won't be long. Bye. (*He clicks off the phone and goes to the desk of the hotel.*)

*Clerk:* May I help you, sir?

*Rob:* Yes. Perhaps. I have here . . . I mean, I found this wallet last night. I was coming across the street with this friend and we were talking about this paper I'm writing—she was telling me that I need to focus more. But, I'm focused. Don't you think I'm focused?

*Clerk:* Well, do you wear glasses? Maybe if you put your glasses on, you'll see a little clearer.

*Rob:* What are you talking about? I can see perfectly well without them!

(*They stare at each other, Rob squinting.*)

*Clerk:* Never mind. Now, you were saying, you found this wallet. Do you remember where?

*Rob:* I was just telling you. In the street! (*He rolls his eyes and sighs.*)

*Clerk:* Of course, in the street. Was there any identification in it?

*Rob:* Yes, of course and also there was an address.

(*Pause*)

*Clerk:* Would you like to share that little bit of information?

*Rob:* I think it was Sheridan Hall.

*Clerk:* Oh no, then you are in the wrong place. It's just down the street. This is the Sheraton Hotel.

(*Rob marches off to the hotel exit. Walks outside, looks both ways, scratches his head, and reenters the hotel, going back to the clerk.*)

Rob:   Did you say to the right or to the left?

Clerk:   (*Amused*) I don't recall saying anything. You go out and turn right and just keep walking for about five minutes, and then you'll see it on your right. On the same side of the street. Got it? Do you want me to write that down?

Rob:   No, that's ok. Thank you. (*Muttering*) I couldn't read it anyway.

Scene 2

(*The same hotel lobby, about half an hour later. Rob comes back in, still holding the wallet, and goes back to the same clerk.*)

Rob:   Remember me?

Clerk:   It's my duty to remember everyone who asks for my assistance.

Rob:   Oh yes. Very nice. Anyway, I went to Sheridan Hall. I mean, I found it all right, but no one had ever heard of him.

Clerk:   Of whom?

Rob:   Of Hooper!

Clerk:   Hooper who?

Rob:   The person who lost this wallet.

Clerk:   Aha! Now I understand. Are you sure you have the right name? Hooper, did you say?

Rob:   Of course. Are you suggesting I cannot read?

Clerk:   Not at all. But these things do happen. I've seen a lot of misunderstanding in my time behind this desk. It's good to just double-check everything. Would you mind if I looked in the wallet? Maybe I'll find something that you overlooked. Two great minds are better than one.

Rob:   Well (*He clutches the wallet to him, but then he decides to hand it to the clerk.*) I suppose I can trust you.

Clerk:   (*He looks in the wallet and pulls out a big wad of money, a driver's license, and a hotel electronic key.*) It says here on the key, "The Sheraton Hotel."

*Rob:*   It does? Are you sure? That's great! I *have* come to the right place.

*Clerk:*   Indubitably, sir!

*Rob:*   So, and this license says Mr. Hooper, right? (*He squints at the license.*)

*Clerk:*   (*Amused*) I'm afraid not, sir. This wallet belongs to a Mr. Kent Cooper. Who happens to be staying at this hotel as we speak.

*Rob:*   That's wonderful (*Clerk nods yes*) And he hasn't left yet? (*Clerk nods no*) That's even better.

*Clerk:*   Why don't you deliver it to him in person? I think he's the kind of gentleman who would offer a generous reward. I'll just buzz his room.

*Rob:*   (*Looking rather embarrassed, he rushes for the exit. Shouts*) You give it to him. I have to be someplace. (*In his hurry, he drops his own wallet.*)

*Clerk:*   (*Notices the wallet and runs toward the door*). Sir! Wait! You've dropped your wallet!

# The Elevator

## *Abnormal situation*

(*An elevator door. A lady, dressed in office clothes, is waiting to get into the elevator. She is looking at her watch and looks nervous. The elevator arrives and suddenly a man, dressed in casual business clothes, comes running into the elevator in front of her. Both get in, but she is rather put out by his rudeness. A lady, also dressed in business clothes, smiles at the man as he gets into the elevator, he smiles back. The elevator continues and the lady who was first in the elevator looks at the floor. The other lady and the man look above the door to see which floor they are on. Suddenly, the man looks at his watch and looks very worried—he presses the stop button. The elevator stops and all three are jolted.*)

*Lady 2:* Hey! What do you think you're doing?

*Man:* I'm terribly sorry, but I have a meeting in fifteen minutes on the seventh floor and I haven't had any lunch yet— I'm starving!

*Lady 2:* Well, that's your problem!

*Man:* (*Searching in his bag, he brings out a small tablecloth, three napkins, and three sandwiches.*) Look, I'm willing to share my lunch with you. See, I have enough for three people.

*Lady 1:* Well, I'm not in a terrible hurry and I am a bit hungry. Oh, why not!

*Lady 2:* (*Quietly to Lady 1*) Are you mad? Don't encourage him! He's a nut! He's probably just been released from the local loony bin! Who knows what he has planned for us!

*Lady 1:* (*Quietly to Lady 2*) Oh, don't be silly! He's perfectly harmless. He's just being nice.

*Lady 2:* Nice?! Yes, he'll be nice until he pulls out a knife and kills us!

*Man:* Ladies, ladies! Relax! I don't have much time for my lunch, never mind a serial killing!

*Lady 2:* You know, it's very rude to listen in on other people's private conversations!

*Man:* (*To both ladies*) Come on, what will it be? Turkey or cheese?

*Lady 1:* Oh, turkey please. Thank you!

*Man:* You're very welcome. (*To Lady 2*) I've heard cheese helps cure paranoia! Here you are! (*He holds out a cheese sandwich to her.*)

*Lady 2:* I wouldn't eat that if you paid me!

*Man:* Oh well, suit yourself. I don't have time to argue. I have a very important meeting to attend.

(*The man and Lady 1 eat their sandwiches. Lady 2 moves to far corner and looks impatient.*)

*Lady 1:* Do you work for the computer firm on the seventh floor?

*Man:* Not exactly...

*Lady 2:* He doesn't work anywhere! He spends his time bothering defenseless women in elevators! Look, will you hurry up! I have a meeting with a very important person in ten minutes. Press that button immediately, or I'll call security!

*Man:* Okay! Okay! (*He presses the button and the elevator moves. He cleans up the mess.*) So who's this very important person you're meeting?

*Lady 2:* (*In a haughty voice*) You won't have heard of him—Bill Gates [*or name of famous person*].

*Man:* (*He suppresses a smile.*) Bill who?

*Lady 2:* Why did I bother? (*The elevator arrives at the seventh floor.*) At last, the seventh floor!

*Man:* Well this is where I'll be getting off too. Nice having lunch with you two ladies! (*He shakes hands with Lady 1 and hands her a business card.*) I'm Bill Gates. It was a pleasure to meet you! Don't hesitate to call me if you need anything!

*Lady 2's face drops. She quickly runs out of the elevator before Bill Gates. She is horrified at her mistake!*

# Blind Date

*A middle-aged man is sitting in a restaurant wearing dark glasses and a carnation in his lapel. He is sitting at a table for two. He looks around hopefully. Whenever a lady comes in, he watches every move and gesture she makes. He is always so disappointed when each lady finds her date.*

*Finally, a middle-aged lady comes in wearing sunglasses and holding a carnation. She cannot see well in her dark glasses, so she crashes into a table and goes up to two other men before she finds the main male character.*

*Lady:*   (*Speaking in a shaky voice*) Are you—tall, dark, handsome, loves romantic dinners for two, and long, brisk walks in the countryside?

*Man:*   Yes, that's me! Are you—bright, loving, enjoys walking by the sea, and has a passion for canaries?

*Lady:*   Yes! May I sit down?

*Man:*   Of course!

(*She feels her way to the chair and finally manages to sit down.*)

*Man:*   Well . . . !

*Lady:*   Well . . . !

*Man:*   Isn't this nice?

*Lady:*   Yes, it is rather.

*Man:*   This is my favorite restaurant.

*Lady:*   Is it? It's very nice.

*Man:*   They have great seafood.

*Lady:*   Oh, do they?

*Man:*   Do you like seafood?

*Lady:*   Erm, actually no—I break out in a rash when I eat it.

*Man:*   Oh, dear.

*Lady:*   Yes . . .

(*They sit in uncomfortable silence for a moment. She fiddles with her napkin and he fidgets in his chair.*)

*Man:*   Did you have any trouble finding the restaurant?

*Lady:*   (*Her voice changes slightly, she starts speaking without*

139

*taking a breath*) Well . . . I thought it would be easy, well, I said to my husband it would be no problem. Well, he's always worrying whether I'll make it to these things on time or not. (*The man starts looking a bit worried and unsure.*) I've never really been able to get anywhere on time—ever since I was a child. You know even my first teacher noticed that I could never get anywhere. . . .

Man: (*Uncomfortable*) Excuse me, but . . . erm. Did I hear you correctly? Did you say, . . . your "husband"?

Lady: (*Matter of fact*) Oh yes, Ernie, that's my husband, he always laughs about my being late. And then there's the forgetfulness. You know I was at the end of the street when . . .

Man: Sorry, but does your husband know you're here . . . with a . . . strange man . . . now?

Lady: Oh yes! Of course, he does . . . silly! Anyway, where was I . . . oh yes, I was at the end of the street when I suddenly realized I was wearing my bedroom slippers and I'd forgotten the carnation and sunglasses. So Ernie, he's such a dear, he came running, well, not exactly running—he's not as young as he used to be, you know—he came running down the road after me with my shoes, the dark glasses, and the flower!

Man: (*Looking very uncomfortable*) He knows you are out on a blind date?

Lady: Yes, of course! Do you think I keep secrets from my husband or something? Oh no, we don't have any secrets, we don't.

Man: (*Feeling extremely confused*) But does he mind? I mean . . . you . . . going out . . . with another . . . man . . . on a . . . blind date? Alone?

Lady: Ernie? No, of course not, silly. Well, he says, "Ethel," he says, that's my name. "Ethel," he says, "you go out and make some friends—you must get so tired of only seeing my face around the place."

Man: (*A little impatiently*) Look, I don't understand. You mean to tell me he encourages you to go on blind dates?

Lady: Well, of course!

*Man:* (*Losing his temper*) Do you or this so-called husband of yours have any idea what a blind date is for? You know, usually single men and women meet each other in order to form a close friendship, possibly even to marry eventually. So, I just don't understand what kind of relationship you and your husband have, but I must say it sounds rather strange to me. And I don't intend to find out, so you can tell this Ernie that I walked out on you! Goodbye!

(*The man storms out of the restaurant. The lady pulls out a cellular phone.*)

*Lady:* (*Speaking with a different voice—younger and more confident than before*) Hello, darling, it's me! Yes, I met another one who fell for it! (*She takes off a wig and the dark glasses to reveal a young attractive woman.*) I got all his credit cards and his wallet. I'll meet you here in ten minutes. See you then. (*She puts the phone away and signals to a waiter who is passing by.*) Waiter, I'll have the best bottle of champagne in the house! Oh, and bring two glasses, I'm expecting company!

## In a Bar

*A bar/disco, a beautiful lady is sitting at the bar and a handsome man (Man 1) is sitting at the other end of the bar. She is having a drink and trying to steal glances at him to see if he is interested in her. He holds up a glass in a toast to her.*

*A second man (Man 2) walks up to the woman. He is holding a notebook. He stands between the Woman and Man 1.*

| | |
|---|---|
| *Man 2:* | (*Reading from his notebook*) What's a lovely woman like you doing in a place like this? |
| *Woman:* | I'm waiting for my seven-foot boyfriend who has a black belt in karate. |
| *Man 2:* | Ha! Ha! Ha! That's very funny—yes I like that. (*Looking through his notebook, then reads.*) Do you have the time? |
| *Woman:* | (*Irritated, she sighs*) No I don't! |
| *Man 2:* | (*He flicks though his book once more and finds another line. Looking pleased with himself, he reads his new line like a grand speech. He holds out the arm not holding the notebook as if addressing a crowd.*) Of all the bars in all the world, you happened to step into this one, sweetheart! (*He grins expectantly at her.*) |
| *Woman:* | (*She rolls her eyes up to heaven in disgust.*) Look, what exactly do you want? You are beginning to annoy me! |
| *Man 2:* | Well, I was hoping we could go out together and maybe it would become a meaningful relationship with a view to marriage. |
| *Woman:* | Well, you're not even going to find a meaningless relationship if you carry on using those lines! |
| *Man 2:* | (*He looks devastated.*) But in my book, *Chat-Up Lines for Dummies*, it says that these lines can never fail. Oh no, now it looks like I've just made you angry. Oh dear! |
| *Woman:* | (*Feeling sorry for him*) Look, I don't want to be mean, but you're just not my type and well, frankly, I don't think I'm your type either. |
| *Man 2:* | (*Sits on a bar stool beside her looking very depressed*) Well, I might as well just give up and go back to stamp collecting! |

*Woman:*    Look, I didn't mean to hurt your feelings and you seem like a nice person. . . . I'd like to help you so that you can meet a nice woman.

*Man 2:*    You mean you want to help me? Oh, thank you! Thank you! Thank you! (*He kisses her hand.*)

*Woman:*    (*Embarrassed*) Calm down will you! Now have a drink and I'll give you a few lessons.

(*He gets a drink from the barman/barmaid*)

*Woman:*    Now you see that handsome guy over there?

*Man 2:*    Yeah!

*Woman:*    Well, I'm going to use him as an example. I'll use a few chat-up techniques on him and you'll see what to do when you see a lady you like. Okay?

*Man 2:*    That sounds great!

*Woman:*    Right. First I need to make some kind of introduction to get a conversation going. I know, I'll ask him for a light.

(*She gets out a cigarette and Man 2 instinctively goes to light it for her. She waves away his lighter and points to Man 1. Man 2 suddenly remembers why she took the cigarette out and puts his notebook and a pen on the bar. She goes over to Man 1.*)

*Woman:*    Excuse me, do you have a light?

*Man 1:*    Sure I do, especially for a lovely lady like you.

*Woman:*    Thank you! (*Man 1 lights her cigarette for her.*) Excuse me one moment, I'll be right back.

(*She goes back to Man 2.*)

*Woman:*    You see he's interested in me now, so the next step is to find out more about him. I'll pretend I've met him somewhere before. If he agrees, it means he's interested, but if he disagrees then that's my cue to give up.

*Man 2:*    (*Writing*) "Cue to give up." How do you spell *cue*?

*Woman:*    "C-U", oh, never mind that, just watch what I do, okay?

(*She goes back to Man 1.*)

*Woman:*    Sorry to bother you, but haven't we met somewhere before? I can't quite remember where . . .

*Man 1:*     You know now that you mention it, yes, I think we have. Remember you dropped a packet of cookies in the supermarket. I picked them up for you!

*Woman:*     Oh, that was you! Well, I think I was so flustered at the time that I forgot to thank you. I just wanted to get out of there after making such a fool . . .

*Man 1:*     Do you live around here?

*Woman:*     Yes, I live around the corner from that supermarket, on Elm Street.

*Man 1:*     What a coincidence, I live on Oak—that's just across the park from you.

*Woman:*     I don't think I've ever seen you there.

*Man 1:*     I've just moved into the area and I'm still trying to get to know the neighborhood.

*Woman:*     Well, I've been here for a long time—I can show you around—if you'd like? Do you see that fellow over there, we were talking earlier and I forgot to tell him something.

(*She goes back to Man 2.*)

*Man 2:*     Well, how's it going?

*Woman:*     Really well! He hasn't been here long and he lives really close to me. I've offered to show him around the area.

*Man 2:*     So what's the next step? Will he ask you out?

*Woman:*     Yes, we're working on that right now!

*Man 2:*     (*Writing*) So where is he taking you?

*Woman:*     Nowhere pretentious, probably some small romantic cozy Italian restaurant.

*Man 2:*     Italian? (*His eyes light up and he writes vigorously.*)

*Woman:*     Now just keep watching.

(*She goes back to Man 1.*)

(*The bartender, who has been reading the newspaper, comes over to Man 2.*)

*Bartender:*     (*Speaking to Man 2, but Man 2 is very busy writing in his notebook while the bartender speaks to him*) Listen to this! A woman held up the bank down the street. People saw her running in this direction, and then she disappeared. They say she had platinum blond hair— you know like Marilyn Monroe—and glasses. It says here that she was wearing (*describe in detail the clothes worn by the actress playing the Woman.*)

(*The bartender looks at the woman while reading the description of the robber in the paper and notices that she fits the description. At each detail he looks at her.*)

Bartender: (*Almost to himself*) But no blond hair or glasses. (*Looking at the woman*) No, it can't be—she's too nice! (*Speaking to Man 2*) What do you think?

Man 2: (*Looking up from his notebook*) What are you talking about? Sorry, my mind was elsewhere.

Bartender: Oh, never mind! Do you want another drink pal?

(*At the other end of the bar, the woman is talking to Man 1.*)

Woman: Would you like me to help you get acquainted with this area? Maybe we could discuss the important landmarks over dinner . . . somewhere?

Man 1: Oh, that would be very nice, could you suggest a nice restaurant?

Woman: I know a lovely Italian restaurant—Marco's On The Park. Have you been there yet?

(*Man 1 looks very thoughtful and repeats the name to himself.*)

Man 1: (*Quietly*) Marco's . . . Marco's, yes I've heard of it. Marco Gianelli.

Woman: (*Looking rather surprised*) Yes, that's right, but how do you know the owner's name?

Man 1: (*Quickly thinking of a good answer*) Oh, well . . . I read about the restaurant in a guidebook and they talked about the owner of that restaurant. Anyway, tell me about yourself. Where do you work? What do you do in your free time? I want to know everything about you!

Woman: (*Looking pleased*) Oh . . . erm . . . Would you excuse me a moment? I just need to tell my friend something.

Man 1: Of course.

(*The woman goes back to talk to Man 2. Man 1 watches her very carefully as she talks to Man 2.*)

Man 2:     Well, is he interested? It looks good from here!

Woman:     Yes, we're going to the Italian restaurant and now he wants to know all about me!

Man 1:     (*A little envious*) You lucky thing! How did you manage that? I wish I were so lucky!

Woman:     Oh, don't worry; you will be! Now it's very important that you observe the last part of my routine.

(*She goes back to Man 1.*)

Man 1:     Now where were we? Oh yes, I remember. May I ask your name?

Woman:     It's Marjorie Thisisastickup.

Man 1:     What a delightful name. How did you get that name?

Woman:     Well, my father was a bank rob . . . a bank manager and there was a robbery the day I was born, so he named me after the words of the robber!

Man 1:     Tell me all about yourself.

Woman:     I'm the manager of my own finance company. A very successful company, I might add!

Man 1:     (*With great interest*) How many employees do you have?

Woman:     Well, that depends on how busy I am. On some days, I need more help than on others, especially on larger jobs. Marco Gianelli helps me with transportation very often and you see that guy over there? (*She points to Man 2.*) He helps me with security. Security is very important in my business.

Man 1:     Where do you normally work?

Woman:     In the local area—my office is in my house.

Man 1:     (*He stands up and takes an identification card from his pocket.*) Well Marjorie Thisisastickup, you won't be going home for a while—you see, I'm a police officer (*he shows her his ID card*) and you are under arrest for the robbery of the bank up the street. (*He puts handcuffs on her.*) We have been tracking you and your friend Gianelli for a while. The missing link was the gun supplier, but now I know who was responsible for the weapons—that friend of yours at the end of the bar!

(*He grabs Man 2 and puts handcuffs on him.*)

Man 1: (*Speaking to Man 2*) You are under arrest for the robbery of the bank up the road.

Man 2: What? Under arrest? I haven't done anything!

Woman: He's got nothing to do with it, he was just trying to chat me up, and you see I was showing him how to chat someone up by chatting you up because he was so bad at it and . . . you've got to believe me!

Man 1: Can't you think of a better story than that?

Woman: But it's true!

Man 1: Tell that to the judge! Come on you two, outside!

(*He takes the woman and Man 2 outside. Man 2 is very shocked indeed!*)

© 2002 by Ann F. Burke and Julie O'Sullivan from *Stage by Stage*. Portsmouth, NH: Heinemann.

# Annotated Bibliography

In this annotated bibliography, we have listed books that we have used and liked over the years. This is not a complete collection and it contains books that are in print and out-of-print, books published for elementary and high school language teachers, ESL/FLT teachers, and books published for actors. We have divided the books into the following categories to make it easier for you to find what you are looking for: theory; drama in schools; activities, games, and role-play; actors' exercises, improvisation, and scripts; playwriting; directing a play; pronunciation; and audio references. In addition, we have coded each entry and added a short description of each book. At the end of the bibliography is a list of indexes and play catalogs where you can find lists of plays.

## Code to Describe Book Entries:

NS = native speaker

ESL/FLT = English as a second language/foreign language teaching

Ch = Children

Teen = Teenagers

Ad = Adults

Ex = Exercises

Scr =Scripts

Imp =Improvisation

P =Pronunciation

PD = Play Directing

PW = Playwriting

RP =Role-play

Th = Theory

# Theory

COLE, T. 1963. *Acting: A Handbook of the Stanislavski Method*. New York: Crown Publishers.

NS/Ad/Ex/Th

A series of essays by various theater professionals discussing the Stanislavski method and how they have incorporated it into their theatrical work.

HEATHCOTE, D., AND G. BOLTON. 1995. *Drama for Learning: Dorothy Heathcote's Mantle of the Expert Approach to Education*. Portsmouth, NH: Heinemann.

NS/Ch/Ad/Th

The authors explore how to teach any subject using theatrical methods to "build expertise" in the students. Theory for teachers.

HOLDEN, S. 1981. *Drama in Language Teaching*. Harlow: Longman.

ESL/FLT/Ch/Teen/Ad/Th

Book is in two major sections. The first is theory and the second is application. Short book: a few ideas for improvisation, for working with pictures or a text. Includes short scripts: *The Party, Silence, A Slight Ache*.

JOHNSON, L., AND C. O'NEILL, eds. 1984. *Dorothy Heathcote Collected Writings on Education and Drama*. London: Hutchinson and Co. Ltd.

NS/Ch/Teen/Th

Theoretical writings and thoughts about drama. Very accessible to the novice teacher of drama.

LANDY, R. 1988. *Handbook of Educational Drama and Theatre*. Westport: Greenwood Press.

NS/Ch/Teen/Ad/Th

It is a good starting point as it provides an overview to different aspects of using drama in education: Educational drama in schools, drama in the community, the theater and children, using puppets.

MOFFETT, J. 1967. *Drama: What Is Happening; the Use of Dramatic Activities in the Teaching of English*. Champaign: National Council of Teachers of English.
NS/Th
A short book about drama theory. Easy to read.

MUSE, I. 1996. *Oral and Nonverbal Expression*. Larchmont: Eye on Education.
NS/Th
See Chapter 3 on understanding and using nonverbal behavior.

## Drama in Schools

ALLEN, J. P. 1979. *Drama in Schools: Its Theory and Practice*. London: Heinemann Educational.
NS/Ch/Th
Background reading for teachers who want to use drama with children. Very theoretical.

CRESCI, M. 1989. *Creative Dramatics for Children (Grades 3–6)*. Glenview: Scott Foresman and Company.
NS/Ch/Ex
Excellent book full of activities. Aimed at children, but many activities can be used for or adapted for older children and adults.

DUKE, C. R. 1974. *Creative Dramatics and English Teaching*. Urbana: National Council of Teachers of English.
NS/Ch/Ex/RP/Th
Combination of theory and practice. Good practical classroom activities in Section 3. Handbook of Resources lists poems, short stories, films. It also has an out-of-date but extensive bibliography.

FENNESSEY, S. 2000. *History in the Spotlight*. Portsmouth: Heinemann.
NS/Ch/Teen/Ex/Imp/PW/RP
Practical tips about how to use drama, improvisation, mime, and

storytelling to teach history. The methods could be adapted to teach various subjects. Very creative and practical.

GRIFFITH, P. 1981. *The School Play: A Complete Handbook*. London: Batsford Academic and Educational Limited.
NS/Teen/PW/PD

Practical book with good advice about choosing a play, writing your own play, conducting rehearsals, and preparing for a public performance. Includes practical exercises and a list of plays suitable for high school students.

HEINIG, R. B. 1987. *Creative Drama Resource Book for Kindergarten Through Grade 3*. Englewood Cliffs: Prentice Hall.
NS/Ch/Ex

Contains great resources from stories and poems to use with young children. Includes very practical activities using drama, stories, pantomime, puppets, and improvisation.

HEINIG, R. B. 1987. *Creative Drama Resource Book for Grades 4 Through 6*. Englewood Cliffs: Prentice Hall.
NS/Ch/Ex/Scr

Practical exercises using drama, improvisation, pantomime, puppets, storytelling. Great resources and exercises for young children.

HEINIG, R. B. 1988. *Creative Drama for the Classroom Teacher*. Englewood Cliffs: Prentice Hall.
NS/Ch/Ex

Author begins with simple activities and games, progresses through pantomime, creative story building, and story dramatization.

KING, N.1993. *Storymaking and Drama: An Approach to Teaching Language and Literature at the Secondary and Postsecondary Levels*. Portsmouth: Heinemann.
NS/Teen/Ad/Ex/Imp/PW/RP

A practical approach to creating stories, telling stories, and using drama in the classroom. Clear, practical explanations and exercises.

KIPNIS, L., AND M. GILBERT. c1994. *Have You Ever—Bringing Literature to Life Through Creative Dramatics: Easy to Use Creative Dramatics Lessons for Well-Known Stories and Poems*. Hagerstown: Alleyside Press.
NS/Ch

Encourages teachers to work with children's imaginations, getting them to "live" the stories and poems.

McCaslin, N. 1980. *Creative Drama in the Classroom*. New York: Longman.

NS/Ch/Imp

Ideas to get children to understand literature through play and "participant theater." Includes exercises in improvisation, mime and movement, puppets and masks, circus, and tips for putting on a play and adapting stories to create plays.

O'Neill, C. 1995. *Drama Worlds: A Framework for Process Drama*. Portsmouth: Heinemann.

NS/Ch/Teen/Ad/Ex/Imp/RP

A description of process drama is followed by practical application of this method in the classroom. The ideas are creative and inventive.

Parry, C. 1972. *English Through Drama: A Way of Teaching*. Cambridge: Cambridge University Press.

NS/Ch/Teen

Narrative account of a British teacher acquainting the boys of his school with the arts of the stage. A little outdated—78 rpm records used for sound—amusing.

Peachment, B. 1976. *Educational Drama: A Practical Guide for Students and Teachers*. Plymouth: Macdonald and Evans.

NS/Ch/Teen/RP

How to teach any subject using drama; scenarios to work with are given. Uses teacher's questions to guide group work.

Scher, A., and C. Verrall. 1975. *100+ Ideas for Drama*. Oxford: Heinemann.

NS/Ch/Teen/Ex

Contains very practical exercises for role play and drama. Focus is on children, but many exercises can be used or adapted for teens and adults.

Spolin, V. 1986. *Theater Games for the Classroom: A Teacher's Handbook*. Evanston: Northwestern University Press.

NS/Ch/Teen/Ex/Imp

Teacher and students focus on finding a mutual objective to solve problems; teacher uses side-coaching and evaluation to help direct students. A rehearsal chart is included.

## Activities, Games, and Role-play

DOUGILL, J., AND L. DOHERTY. 1987. *Drama Activities for Language Learning*. London: Macmillan Publishers.

ESL/FLT/Teen/Ad/Ex/Scr/Imp/RP

Full of ideas for using drama activities in a classroom from using role-play exercises to putting on a play.

FINGER, A. G. 2001. *The Magic of Drama: An Oral Performance Activity Book*. Burlingame: Alta Books.

ESL/FLT/Teen/Ad/Ex/RP/Imp

A book containing varied oral and written activities including role-play and improvisation.

GOTEBIOWSKA, A. 1990. *Getting Students to Talk*. Hemel Hempstead: Prentice Hall.

ESL/FLT/Teen/Ad/Ex/RP

Practical role-play exercises with situations and role cards. Nice exercises. A very easy book to read.

HAYES, S. K. 1984. *Drama as a Second Language*. Cambridge: National Extension College Trust Ltd.

ESL/FLT/Teen/Ad/Ex/Scr/Th/Imp/PD

An excellent out-of-print book with many suggestions for classroom activities. The book focuses on voice, movement, mime, and improvisation exercises. The explanations are clear and practical.

HOETKER, J. 1975. *Theater Games: One Way into Drama*. Urbana: National Council of Teachers of English: ERIC Clearinghouse on Reading and Communication Skills.

NS/Ex

Not a big book, but some interesting activities and a few references at the back. Eleven pages of practical theory—the book refers frequently to Viola Spolin's *Improvisation for the Theater*.

KAO, S., AND C. O'NEILL. 1998. *Words into Worlds: Learning a Second Language Through Process Drama*. Greenwich: Ablex.

ESL/FLT/Teen/Ad

Students build ideas, negotiate, and respond in the target language. Surprise is the key element.

KELLER, B. 1975. *Taking Off: A Practical Handbook for Teachers of Creative Drama*. Vancouver: November House.

NS/Teen/Ad/Ex

Very practical small handbook full of activities. References at the
back to music that can be used with the activities in the book.

LADOUSSE, G. P. 1987. *Role Play*. Oxford: Oxford University Press.

ESL/FLT/Teen/Ad/Ex/RP

Very practical dip-into book. Lots of role-play and speaking exercises that are labeled very clearly to help the teacher choose
an exercise quickly.

LANNING, C. C. 1997. *Creative Dramatics in the Classroom*. Rocky
River: The Center for Learning.

NS/Teen/Ad/Ex/RP

A book in three parts: vocal expression, body language, and character creation. It is very user-friendly with detailed and clear
descriptions of each activity and provides ready-made handouts for activities. There is a nice, but small, reference section at the back for books, poetry, and short stories.

LEE, W. R. 1979. *Language Teaching Games and Contests*. Oxford:
Oxford University Press.

ESL/FLT/Teen/Ad/Ex/RP

Contains language games and role-play exercises.

MACDONALD, M., AND S. ROGERS-GORDON. 1984. *Action Plans*. Boston:
Heinle & Heinle.

ESL/FLT/Teen/Ex

Eighty student-centered language activities that were developed at
the School for International Training in Brattleboro, Vermont.
Part III is Theater Techniques.

MALEY, R., AND A. DUFF. 1982. *Drama Techniques in Language Learning: A Resource Book of Communication Activities for Language Teachers*. Cambridge: Cambridge University Press.

ESL/FLT/Teen/Ad/Ex/RP

Nonverbal games are useful for relaxation and body movement
exercises. Many verbal activities for all levels of language
learning. Not about putting on a play.

MORGAN, J., AND M. RINVOLUCRI. 1988. *Once Upon a Time: Using Stories in the Language Classroom*. Cambridge: Cambridge University Press.

ESL/FLT/Teen/Ad/Ex/RP

Hands-on storytelling exercises.

PHILLIPS, S. 1999. *Drama with Children*. Oxford: Oxford University Press.

ESL/FLT/Ch/Ex/RP

Practical ideas for using drama with children in the language classroom.

RINVOLUCRI, M. 1984. *Grammar Games: Cognitive, Affective, and Drama Activities for EFL Students*. Cambridge: Cambridge University Press.

ESL/FLT/Teen/Ad/Ex

A selection of grammar games for communication.

SADOW, S. A. 1982. *Idea Bank: Creative Activities for the Language Class*. Rowley: Newbury House Publishers, Inc.

ESL/FLT/Teen/Ad/Ex

Activities to practice communicative skills. Author suggests small-group work (less interference from the teacher). Objectives, preactivity preparation, discussion questions, and writing topics are included.

SMITH, S. M. 1984. *The Theater Arts and the Teaching of Second Languages*. Reading: Addison-Wesley Pub. Co.

ESL/FLT/Teen/Ad/Ex/RP/Imp/PD

Very practical exercises and productions to help you and your students put on a play.

WHITESON, V. 1996. *New Ways in Using Drama and Literature in Language Teaching*. Waldorf: TESOL Publications.

NS/Ch/Teen/Ad/Ex/RP

A collection of exercises for incorporating drama, stories, and poetry into the second language classroom.

WOLF, A. 1990. *Something Is Going to Happen: Poetry Alive!* Ashville: IAMBIC Publications.

NS/Ch/Teen/Ad/Ex

A book written by the company Poetry Alive! that takes poetry performance to schools across the United States. The book explains how to perform poetry to children. It is very practical and contains a number of poems for more than one voice.

## Actors' Exercises, Improvisation, and Scripts

ATKINS, G. 1994. *Improv! A Handbook for the Actor*. Portsmouth: Heinemann.

NS/Teen/Ad/Ex/Imp

This is a book for actors who are interested in improvisation, but has ideas that are appropriate for ESL classrooms.

BERNARDI, P. 1992. *Improvisation Starters: A Collection of 900 Improvisation Situations for the Theater*. White Hall: Betterway Publications.

NS/Teen/Ad/Imp

For each situation, the scene is described and the characters' objectives are given. Good conflict situations are suggested.

BERT, N. 1987. *One-Act Plays for Acting Students*. Colorado Springs: Meriwether Publishing.

NS/Teen/Ad/Scr

Contains short one-act plays for one, two, or three actors and some notes on rehearsal and performance.

BERT, N., AND D. BERT. 1993. *Play It Again!* Colorado Springs: Meriwether Publishing Ltd.

NS/Ad/Scr/PD

Contains short one-act plays for one, two, or three actors and some notes on rehearsal and performance.

BOAL, A. 1992. *Games for Actors and Non-Actors*. London: Routledge.

NS/Teen/Ad/Ex

Lots of acting exercises.

CARUSO, S., AND P. CLEMENS. 1992. *The Actor's Book of Improvisation*. New York: Penguin Books.

NS/Ad/Imp

Contains source material from movies, plays, novels, news items, etc. Nearly two hundred ideas for one or two actors.

CASE, D., AND K. WILSON. 1995. *English Sketches: Sketches from the English Teaching Theatre Intermediate*. Oxford: Heinemann.

ESL/FLT/Teen/Ad/Scr/DP

Contains fun, short sketches for ESL students with some suggestions for activities and performance.

CASSADY, M. 1985. *The Book of Scenes for Acting Practice*. Lincolnwood: The National Book Company.

NS/Teen/Ad/Scr

Scenes from mostly American plays for one woman, one man, two women, two men, one woman and one man, or three mixed.

CASSADY, M. 1989. *The Book of Cuttings for Acting and Directing.* Lincolnwood: National Textbook Company.
NS/Ad/Scr/PD
The book contains a collection of scenes for one, two, three, or more actors. There are practical suggestions for preparation of these scenes.
CASSADY, M. 1993. *Acting Games: Improvisations and Exercises.* Colorado Springs: Meriwether Publishing.
NS/Teen/Ad/Ex/Scr/Imp
Contains exercises for relaxing and focusing; acting games; improvisations; scripts; and exercises for preparing a performance.
CLEESE, J., AND C. BOOTH. 1989. *The Complete Fawlty Towers.* London: Methuen, Mandarin.
NS/Teen/Ad/Scr
The complete scripts from the British television comedy program *Fawlty Towers.*
DIPIETRO, R. J. 1987. *Strategic Interaction: Learning Languages Through Scenarios.* Cambridge: Cambridge University Press.
ESL/FLT/Teen/Ad/Ex/Imp
Scenarios are situations chosen or created by the teacher. In groups students appraise the situation; consider options to solve it; try to anticipate responses of others; they then interact with another group, improvising dialogue.
DURRELL, D. D., AND B. A. CROSSLEY. 1957. *Thirty Plays for Classroom Reading.* Boston: Plays Inc.
NS/Ch/Scr
Contains scripts for children to read and perform. Before each play, there is a short introduction and an indication of how many male and female roles in the play.
DURRELL, D. D., AND B. A. CROSSLEY. 1971. *Favorite Plays for Classroom Reading.* Boston: Plays Inc.
NS/Ch/Scr
Contains scripts for children to read and perform. Before each play, there is a short introduction and an indication of how many male and female roles in the play.
DURRELL, D. D., AND B. A. CROSSLEY. 1971. *Teen-age Plays for Classroom Reading.* Boston: Plays Inc.
NS//Teen/Scr

Contains scripts for teens to read and perform. Before each play, there is a short introduction and an indication of how many male and female roles in the play.

ELKIND, S. 1992. *Scenes for Acting and Directing*. Studio City: Players Press.

NS/Teen/Ad/Scr

Interesting scenes from major American plays (examples: *All My Sons, A Raisin in the Sun*). Background for each scene is given and in the margins there are questions to aid in interpretation.

FULLEYLOVE, E. 1984. *Starting Points for Drama*. Banbury: Kemble Press.

NS/Ch/Ad/Ex

Very practical. A few warm-up exercises. Each chapter contains a very short story for children with pre- and post-reading improvisation exercises. Stories could be used for performance.

GOLDBERG, A. 1991. *Improv Comedy*. Hollywood: Samuel French.

NS/Teen/Ad/Ex/Imp

Comic situations for improvisation practice.

HALPERN, D. 1991. *Plays in One-Act*. New Jersey: The Ecco Press.

NS/Ad/Ex/Scr

Short one-act plays by leading playwrights.

HEWITT, L., AND P. BERNAL. 1995. *Spotlight Plays for the ESOL Classroom*. New York: McGraw Hill.

ESL/FLT/Ch/Teen/Ad/Scr

This series of four titles contains four plays adapted from famous literary stories for ESL learners. The teacher's edition contains notes on producing each play.

HUGO, B., ed. 1988/1989. *Spotlight: A Collection of One-Act Plays for Active Participants*. Pretoria: Jager-Haum.

NS/Ad/Scr

A collection of five one-act plays with some suggestions for reading the play followed by discussion questions.

JESSE, A. 1996. *The Playing Is the Thing*. Burbank: Wolf Creek Press.

NS/Teen/Ad/Ex

Acting games and exercises.

MCCALLUM, G. P. 1976. *Six Stories for Acting*. Culver City: ESL Publications.

ESL/FLT/Teen/Ad/Scr

Six short plays for reading aloud in upper-intermediate levels of English as a Second Language. Reading comprehension questions follow each play.

McCallum, G. P. 1977. *Seven Plays from American Literature*. Culver City: ELS Publications.

ESL/FLT/Teen/Ad/Scr

Short plays adapted from nineteenth-century American literature, requiring only about fifteen minutes to perform. Reading comprehension questions follow each play.

McRae, J. 1985. *Using Drama in the Classroom*. Oxford: Pergamon Institute of English.

ESL/FLT/Teen/Ad/Ex /Scr

The book is divided into two parts: the first part contains a description of how to use drama in the classroom. The second part has scenes from well-known plays and notes on performing these scenes. A very practical book with good scene extracts.

Muir, F., and S. Brett. 1982. *The Penguin Book of Comedy Sketches*. London: Penguin Books.

NS/Teen/Ad/Scr

Short British comedy sketches.

Myles, J. 2002. *Timesaver Photocopiable Plays*. Burlingame: Alta Books.

ESL/FLT/Teen/Scr

This book contains twelve short plays written for teenagers about situations familiar to them.

Nicholas, A. 1990. *99 Film Scenes for Actors*. New York: Avon Books.

NS/Teen/Ad/Scr

Contains scripts of scenes from popular movies.

Olfsen, L., ed. 1970. *50 Great Scenes for Student Actors*. New York: Bantam Books.

NS/Teen/Ad/Scr

Scenes for two actors from plays by well-known playwrights.

Polsky, M. E. 1998. *Let's Improvise: Becoming Creative, Expressive & Spontaneous Through Drama*. 3rd ed. New York: Applause.

NS/Teen/Ad/Imp

An actor's book. Ideas for play-making and story-theater (where a narrator is also a character).

Press, K., ed. 1994. *The World on a Hill and Other Plays*. Cape Town: Oxford University Press.
NS/Teen/Ad/Scr
Contains a number of short plays suitable for high school students. After each play, there are discussion questions and ideas for improvisation. In addition, the introduction offers some suggestions about how to put on a play.

Ratliff, G. L. 1993. *Playing Scenes*. Colorado Springs: Meriwether Publishing Ltd.
NS/Teen/Ad/Scr
A selection of scenes from well-known plays.

Sanders, S. 1970. *Creating Plays with Children*. New York: Citation Press.
NS/Ch/Teen/Scr
Scripts for six short plays based on famous stories—for example, *The Wizard of Oz*. There is a short introduction about writing your own script and dramatizing it.

Self, D., ed. 1980. *Situation Comedy*. London: Hutchinson and Co.
NS/Teen/Ad/Scr
Contains scripts from British BBC TV comedy programs with some suggestions about how to use the scripts in class.

Shackleton, M. 1985. *Double Act: Ten One-Act Plays on Five Themes*. London: Edward Arnold.
ESL/FLT/Teen/Ad/Scr
Ten short plays selected for high-intermediate learners of English as a second language. Includes a glossary and helpful ideas on how to stage these plays if the class so desires.

Spolin, V. 1963. *Improvisation for the Theater: A Handbook of Teaching and Directing Techniques*. Evanston: Northwestern University Press.
NS/Ch/Teen/Ex/Scr/Imp
The teacher and the children must decide on a mutual objective to give focus to the exercises. Teacher's tools: side-coaching and evaluation.

Stanley, S. M. 1980. *Drama Without Script: The Practice of Improvised Drama*. London: Hodder and Stoughton.

NS/Ch/Teen/Ex/Imp/RP

Lots of easy-to-follow exercises and practical information about putting on a play. Some helpful resources at the back.

VIA, R. A. 1976. *English in Three Acts*. East-West Center: The University Press of Hawaii.

ESL/FLT/Teen/Ad/Ex/Scr/PD

This is a wonderful book, out-of-print and never easy to come by, but if you find it, put it in your library. It does everything that we want to do in our book and is a pleasure to read as well.

VIA, R. A., AND L. E. SMITH. 1983. *Talk and Listen: English as an International Language via Drama Techniques*. Oxford: Pergamon Press.

ESL/FLT/Teen/Ad/Ex/Scr

This book contains paired incomplete short dialogues. The lines for B are on the back of the page that contains the lines for A, so that neither A nor B can see what the other is saying; they must listen to each other. The final lessons (21–30) are situations for improvisations.

WEST, C., ed. 2000. *Oxford Bookworm Playscripts*. Oxford: Oxford University Press.

ESL/FLT/Teen/Ad/Scr

This series includes graded play scripts of classic plays, such as *Romeo and Juliet* and *The Importance of Being Earnest*. The scripts are accompanied by performance notes.

WINTHER, B. 1976. *Plays from Folktales of Africa and Asia*. Boston: Plays Inc.

NS/Teen/Ad/Scr

One-act plays (royalty-free) for young people based on African and Asian folktales.

YOUNG, G., ed. 2000. *The Best American Short Plays*. New York: Applause Books.

NS/Teen/Ad/Scr

This is a series of books containing scripts of a number of plays.

## Playwriting

BRAY, E. 1994. *Playbuilding*. Portsmouth: Heinemann.

NS/Ch/Teen/Imp/PW

A guide for group creation of plays with young people through improvisation, discussion, and rehearsal.

CASSADY, M. 1984. *Playwriting Step-by-Step*. San Jose: Resource Publications, Inc.

NS/Teen/PW

A very detailed book on how to develop characters, plot, and action, as well as how to build sets and market a performance.

NORTON, J. H., AND F. GRETTON. 1972. *Writing Incredibly Short Plays, Poems, Stories*. New York: Harcourt Brace Jovanovich, Inc.

NS/Teen/Ad/PW

Shows how to write plays one step at a time: where a playwright must begin and how to develop conflict and consequences.

WESSELS, C. 1993. "From Improvisation to Publication Through Drama." In *Methods That Work*, ed. J. W. Oller, Jr., 368–373. Boston: Heinle & Heinle.

Contains a one-page questionnaire to get a class improvising and writing a play.

## Directing a Play

CURRY, J. 1980. *Amateur Theatre*. Sevenoaks: Hodder and Stoughton.

NS/Teen/Ad/Ex/DP

Contains practical advice about putting on a play with an amateur theater group.

LEGAT, M. 1984. *Putting on a Play*. New York: St. Martin's Press.

NS/Ad/Ex/DP

Practical suggestions for putting on a play.

MCCASLIN, N. 1979. *Shows on a Shoestring: An Easy Guide to Amateur Productions*. New York: David McKay Company Inc.

NS/Ch/Ad/DP

Gives guidelines to the director of an amateur group to put on a play. Contains good, practical advice for short, simple performances.

## Pronunciation

CICELY B. 1973. *Voice and the Actor*. New York: Macmillan.

163

NS/Ex/P

The book contains explanations of how physically to pronounce English sounds. It has pronunciation exercises and poems for reading practice.

DAUER, R. M. 1993. *Accurate English*. New Jersey: Regents/Prentice Hall.

ESL/FLT/Ex/P

Practical pronunciation exercises focusing on different aspects of English pronunciation. The focus is on American English.

FLEISCHMAN, P. 1989. *Phoenix Rising: Poems for Two Voices*. New York: HarperCollins.

NS/Ch/Teen/P

A collection of wonderful poems for two voices. Great for performance or for stress, intonation, and rhythm exercises.

FLEISCHMAN, P. 1992. *Joyful Noise: Poems for Two Voices*. New York: HarperCollins.

NS/Ch/Teen/P

A collection of wonderful poems for two voices. Great for performance or for stress, intonation, and rhythm exercises.

GRAHAM, C. 2001. *Jazz Chants Old and New*. Oxford: Oxford University Press.

ESL/FLT/Ch/Teen/Ad/Ex/P

Fun exercises for practicing stress, rhythm, and intonation.

KENWORTHY, J. 1987. *Teaching English Pronunciation*. Harlow: Longman.

ESL/FLT/Ex/P

Guidelines on teaching pronunciation for teachers as well as exercises for students. The last part of the book outlines common pronunciation problems of learners from different countries.

MORTIMER, C. 1985. *Elements of Pronunciation*. Cambridge: Cambridge University Press.

ESL/FLT/Ex/P

Practical pronunciation exercises each focusing on a different aspect of English pronunciation. The focus is on British English.

PARROTT, E. 1983. *The Penguin Book of Limericks*. London: Penguin.

NS/Ad/P

A large collection of very amusing limericks.

SWAN, M., AND B. SMITH. 1987. *Learner English*. Cambridge: Cambridge University Press.
ESL/FLT/P
A very useful reference book that outlines the pronunciation problems faced by learners of English with specific native languages.

## Audio References

BBC. 1991. *The BBC Sound Effects Library* [CD set]. Princeton: Films for the Humanities and Sciences.
Sixty disk set of 2,250 sound effects.

## Indexes and Catalogs of Plays

CONNOR, B. M., AND H. G. MOCHEDLOVER. 1988. *Ottemiller's Index to Plays in Collections 7th ed*. Metuchen: The Scarecrow Press.
An author–title index to plays appearing in collections published between 1900 and 1985.

*Dramatists Play Service Complete Catalogue of Plays and Musicals*. New York: Dramatists Play Service, Inc.
Complete catalogue in even years; supplement in odd years. Indexed by authors and by titles.

IRELAND, N. O. 1958. *An Index to Skits and Stunts*. Boston: F. W. Faxon Company, Inc.

KELLER, D. H. 1990. *Index to Plays in Periodicals*. Metuchen: The Scarecrow Press, Inc.

LOGASA, H., AND W. VER NOOY. 1924–1955. *Index to One-Act Plays*. 4 vols. Boston: F.W. Faxon Company.

LOGASA, H., AND W. VER NOOY. 1966. *Index to One-Act Plays for Stage, Radio, and Television*. Supplement 5. Boston: F. W. Faxon Company.

MERSAND, J. 1988. *Index to Plays with Suggestions for Teaching*. New York: The Scarecrow Press.

PATTERSON, C. 1970. *Plays and Periodicals Index to English Scripts in the Twentieth-Century Journals*. Boston: G.K. Hall & Co.

SAMPLES, G. 1974. *The Drama Scholar's Index to Plays and Filmscripts in Selected Anthologies, Series, and Periodicals*. Metuchen: The Scarecrow Press.

SAMUEL FRENCH, INC. *Basic Catalog of Plays* (see p. 60).

WELCH, J. *Baker's Plays. General Catalogue and Theatre Resource Directory.* Boston: Baker's Plays (published generally in August).

Lists plays from Broadway, Off-Broadway, the West End (London) and the regional theaters of the United States. Each play is briefly described in terms of size and composition of the cast, number of scenes, sets, and plot summary.

YAAKOV, J., AND J. GREENFIELDT. 1953-1998. *Play Index.* New York: H. W. Wilson Co.

YAAKOV, J., AND J. GREENFIELDT, ed. 1998. *Play Index.* New York: The H. W. Wilson Company.

The plays listed are plays published between 1993 and 1997. Plays are listed by author, title, and subject. The author entry is the most complete. Also notes when plays are in collections. In addition, plays are listed by gender and number—that is, 1W plays, 2W plays, etc. Broad scope of types of plays included: plays for Christmas (listed separately), TV or puppet plays, musicals, and classical dramas.

# Websites:

*www.bakersplays.com*
*www.dramatists.com*
*www.samuelfrench.com*
*www.stageplays.com*